GENTLEWOMAN

ETIQUETTE FOR A **LADY**, FROM A GENTLEMAN

Inspired by,

You

Composed by,

Enitan O. Bereola, II

Author of **BEREOLAESQUE**

II

ALSO BY ENITAN O. BEREOLA II:
Award-Winning | Best-Selling Book

BEREOLAESQUE: The Contemporary Gentleman & Etiquette Book for the Urban Sophisticate

Bereolaesque.com

WHAT IMPORTANT PEOPLE ARE SAYING…

"This book reminds society of one thing: women are the greatest creation and should be treated that way."

Hill Harper
Award-winning Actor
New York Times Best-selling Author

*"Lovvvvvvving Gentlewoman!!!! Wowwwwwwww!!!
Wow!!!!! 'Tis the truth and I'm LOVING it!!! This book is sure to inspire!"*

Michelle Williams
Destiny's Child
Grammy Award-winning Singer/Songwriter; Actress;
Philanthropist
1/3 of the Best-Selling Recording Group of all Time

"This is exciting. A lot of people have embraced stuff that really isn't what femininity should be about. Women should be who they are. Women need to be free to determine who they want to be. This book supports that."

Congresswoman Barbara Lee
Member of the U.S. House of Representatives
U.S. Ambassador to United Nations

BOOK COVER CREDITS
Cover Model: Graham Knoxx |
GrahamKnoxx.com
Photographer: Andrew Marshall
MMI Digital Photography |
Cover Editor: Jus10 Huff |

ILLUSTRATION CREDITS
Illustrator: Lindsay Adams
2ndandL.com

PHOTOGRAPHY INSERT CREDITS
Photography: CTRL Studios
Atlanta, GA ctrlstudios.com |
Andrew Marshall MMI Digital
Photography |
Model 1: Chenoia N. Bryant
Model 2: Heather Norton
Model 3: Crystal Hanes
Model 4: Martha Kim
Model 5: Lisa Campbell
Model 6: Graham Knoxx
Model 7: Arie Luster
Model 8: Dorien Toku

Model 9: Jordyn Bullock

PORN FLOWER ART
Conceptual Artist: Bai Yun
Yunbai.com

CONTRIBUTOR CREDITS
Meagan Good
Bryan-Michael Cox
Congresswoman Barbara Lee
Alesha Reneé
Dr. Jamal Bryant
Bobby Wagner
Letisha Bereola
Leola Bell
Luciana Garbarni
Jaye Price
Jerri Evans
Rahman Ray Grayson
Toye Adedipe
Everett Frampton
Idoroenyi Amanam, MD

CREDITS OF INSPIRATION
The Mrs. Bereola

-*"Uneasy lies the head that wears a crown."* –Shakespeare

GENTLEWOMAN.

|ˈJen͵tl-woŏm͵ən |

-noun:

1. Feminine.

2. Rare.

3. Legendary.

4. You.

Reshaping the idea of how ~~men view women and~~ women view themselves.

To
Frettie Jackson,
Who set the standard for class...

To
Gwendolyn Toney,
A woman who bears a child is a mother – you're far greater than that. You're a friend, a teacher, a nurturer and so much more. I've never met anyone like you and never will. I owe you the world, but for now here's this book...

To
Brenda Swann,
A second mother to me, you epitomize sophistication, femininity and strength – and you do it all without effort. You are the standard...

To
L.V.B.,
You are my bridge to God. Everything excessively beautiful in this book is about you. Meet me upstairs, baby! After that, let's go to Paris...

To

A.G. Bereola,

... I didn't create you, but we share the same blood. I was touring the country when you were born into this cold world, but you warmed my heart with the touch of a finger when we met. You were so attentive to the space around you. Your round, watchful eyes wandered back and forth as if you were watching a game of Ping-Pong. Your only concern was milk, naptime and love. Soon, that's all going to change.

You'll begin seeking freedom by learning to walk. You'll gain a sense of beautiful independence learning all by yourself. You don't yet know what planning is, so you'll have the most fun being spontaneous. If you don't get something right, you'll try again and again until it's exactly how you want it. You'll do things your way. Whether you're qualified or not, you'll take risks. You'll be honest and ask a lot of questions. You won't be afraid to express yourself. You'll value relationships and enjoy life's simple pleasures. You won't be too concerned with the real world because your imagination will take you places you've never been. You'll believe in the unbelievable. You'll play in life's discoveries and laugh in the face of its danger. But soon that's all going to change.

Something strange is going to happen. You'll be introduced to this thing called experience. Experience will try to steal your freedom, independence, spontaneity and all those things that made life beautiful as a child. Experience will get you acquainted with doubt and reality. It will try to chip away at your confidence and make you even second-guess your once-so-sure self. Use experience to propel you and keep you safe, but don't let it to steal your zeal.

Don't let "reality" make you lose faith in God and gain faith in man. Don't put your joy in man because when man leaves, there goes your joy. The world didn't give you your joy and the world can't take it away. Your value isn't in the hands of people and your worth was determined when you got here. You were born gorgeous, but the world will try to convince you otherwise. You're the daughter of The King of Kings and your worth extends beyond the clouds. You're a product of love.

You come from a line of many great men, but many men won't hold open your doors unless you hold open your legs. You come from plenty brilliant women, but plenty women will tell you you're not brilliant. Things will get confusing. The world will lie to you and try to take pieces of your beauty. Take ownership of your desires and make your own decisions. Think back to that little girl. Don't forget who you are. Never forget whose you are. You're the most beautiful soul in the world...never change. Wherever you go and whatever you do, we are connected for life.

"Sometimes the king is a woman ..."

— James De La Vega

Judge This Book by its Cover

She's classic. She'll never go out of style. She's particularly presented, well-behaved and well-paid. She's feminine and fashionable, but wears a crooked crown because real Ladies aren't perfect and perfect Ladies aren't real. She works damn hard, owns her own and owns up to who she is. She supersedes elegance. She's a lover of God, good food, good novels and good manners. She has a crush on culture and cocktails. She's confident and intelligent. If you're brave enough to read her, understand her and listen to her advice, you will become her ...

... She is king.

Gentlewoman.

READER DISCLAIMER

The content of this book is exclusively intended for the entity of whom it is addressed. I specifically had you in mind when constructing its invaluable scribing. This book contains confidential or privileged material to be used for the benevolence of womankind. Any unauthorized behavior is prohibited beyond this point. I leave you with the responsibility of transforming literature into lifestyle, impacting this world one gentlewoman at a time. This is not merely a book—but a lifestyle.

—*Bereolaesque*

CONTENTS

...

III

Foreword

To the women,

Who find just as much inspiration in tracing the veins on the back of the curious hands

Of a lover, as they do in tracing their own curves in the full-length mirror.

It's the halves that have us in half,

And in between those cracks we fill with love.

A love that leaks through our lips when we talk about a lover like he put the stars in the sky,

And a self-love to know that without us, there would be no sky.

Luciana Garbarni

Prelude

Hurricane Katrina: *Calm the Storm*

Sometimes the best advice is to ignore advice, including mine. Who do I think I am writing literature for women, anyway? If I were to read this book title in front of a room full of feminists, I might get more *boos* than a polygamist. But wait! Don't shut the book. Listen to my story:

When my siblings were younger, my father locked his keys in the car along with my three-year-old brother. Inconvenient drops of warm, salt-soaked sweat reminded them it was a hot California summer. The car interior was like an oven. It hurt to breathe. Cell phones were non-existent as a casual luxury to call for help – my father began to panic. He tried enlisting the assistance of several strangers in the parking lot, but the world was in a rush that day. As my sister tried to get our father's attention, he scolded her. He frantically searched his pockets for change to use a payphone while she tugged at his waist. "Not now!" father yelled, "This is an emergency." The texture of his voice was like sandpaper. "Well this is an emergency, too!" she thought. Once again, my sister innocently grabbed a handful of his turquoise blue track pants. "Woman," he said calmly. She was only a little girl. She knew he was serious. But if she didn't give it one last attempt, my brother would cook! Finally she yelled, "Tell him to roll down the window from inside the car and you can unlock the door yourself!" They both learned valuable lessons that day:

1. **Drown out the noise. Shatter your bias. When you actually sit quietly and listen, you can learn anything from anyone. If the advice is applicable, then the source is irrelevant. The truth remains the truth whether**

19

accepted or denied and no matter whom it's delivered by. God spoke through an ass (*Numbers 22:28*).

2. **Though opposition might meet you, share your solutions in an emergency. It can save a life.**

Whether right or wrong, some things need to be said in order to start a necessary conversation.

This is an emergency! I don't care if it's popular; I care if it's truth. I didn't write this book because I wanted to, but because I had to. My goal isn't for you to like me; my goal is for you to like yourself. If you're looking for praise without justification, unmerited approval and someone to kiss your ass, you've come across the wrong author. If you're looking for exaggerated, chauvinistic and irrational literature, you've picked up the wrong book. This isn't one of those "how to get a man" books or "I think I'm right just because I'm a man" books.

This is an authentic etiquette book for women, written by a man–a crazy man, crazy over you and crazy enough to write for and about you. I understand that women are natural healers, but you too require healing. It's OK to hurt. You have permission to cry. Your glow is recoverable. It will return. The problem with strength is no one ever asks if you're well. Sometimes you're not OK, and that's OK. Your journey to womanhood is no joke. I've witnessed it through my grandmother's weary eyes, through my mother's silent struggles and through my sister's violent tears. What can I tell you about being a woman? Nothing. That isn't my place. Women experience the world in a way men never will. You have a journey with struggles we won't relate to. But I can remind you who you are. I can provide clarity from an unbiased perspective. I can get you to love yourself more, and men and women to love each other better. I can encourage you on your journey and at your pit stops. I can provide balance. I don't want to change you. I want to add to you. You'll willingly change for yourself.

Much of the information about women is filtered through other women. Don't allow your ears to be impervious to my words because I'm a man. Sometimes you want to hear a guy's thoughts. Do women only listen to women? Do you ignore everything coming from a man because he's a man? Hypersensitivity and political correctness should never drown out truth. Ever. If a fellow handed you one million dollars, would you refuse it because it came from a bloke? A million dollars is still a million dollars, no matter who hands it to you. Its value won't change because a man delivered it. That's a ridiculous notion. I didn't come to pick a fight. Sensitivity was highly considered while producing this literature. The value of its content doesn't change because a man wrote it. This is an emergency!

Pay attention to your story. How's it being told? What's being said? Are you presented accurately? The lines between fact and fiction are blurred. Your truth is watered down. Society is taking notes. A woman's narrative isn't limited to flesh and childbearing. You're more than a victim with hips. Is this your story?

You don't have to take my word for it. This manual is full of real insight from unbiased men, and yes, some women. I've enlisted the help of several friends from celebrities to common folk, doctors and athletes–each contributing to the conversation. All contributions offer perspectives from different walks of life with vast views. This story is the voice of fathers, loving husbands, boyfriends, friends, brothers and sons. It's the voice of your culture and your community.

It's been said the thinnest book in the world is titled, "What Men Know about Women." I'd argue the thinnest book in the world is titled, "Who Cares Enough to Say Anything about the Demise of a Lady?" I'm willing to increase the pages. Each page written to explore, inform, educate and empower.

This book isn't the end all be all. This book is a suggestion. This book is about honesty. Utilize this literature as a reflective piece to reveal what you want to improve upon and what you want to celebrate. I wrote this book to draw you closer to the thoughts you have about yourself – sometimes that's best accomplished from the outside looking in. This literary work isn't intended to judge, it's intended to restore. It wasn't written to be judged, but to be considered.

We'll face every issue head-on. The solutions will heal women. The solutions will heal relationships. The solutions will heal a nation. *Gentlewoman* is the solution. Life starts with a Lady. It starts with you. It starts here. It begins now. Society says there are two kinds of people in this world—well, you aren't either of them. You set the standard. Everything and everyone must adjust to a woman. A gentlewoman.

This is a Ladies' etiquette book from a gentleman's perspective. It's non-fiction. This story is inspired by real events. Whether traditional or contemporary, this story is for you. This story is for the saint and the sinner, although the saint is a sinner. This story is for the Lady with style and grace, and the Lady with absolutely no taste. *Gentlewoman* is for the gentle woman and the tomboy just looking for her place. It's for the misfit and the mannerly. It's for the experienced, just as it's for the virgin. This story is for the sexy, the successful, the humble and the creative–this story is for you. This is for the rude, the ignorant, the misinformed and the shameless–this story is for you. This is for those indifferent and those who don't give a damn. This story is a mirror reflecting society. It's "sugar-free." If you don't like what you see, change it. This isn't written in condemnation, but in compassion. Whatever your story, I crafted this book exclusively for you.

Women have questions. *Gentlewoman* has answers.

Gentlewoman was developed with purpose and is for every woman who strives to live life on purpose. I want readers to find comfort in their individuality and aim to inspire the confidence and courage to be themselves. The greatest gift you can give this world is your authentic self with some manners. My hope is that you apply all that's applicable, neglect what isn't and progress further in humanity because of it. My desire is for you to be more aware of yourself and others. My wish is for you to perpetually fall in love with yourself again, again and again, and all over again.

Capture this book's wisdom. Bask in its good word. Adhere to its value. Laugh at its sarcasm. Ignore its ignorance. Ugly-cry when it's beautiful. Think deeply when it hurts. Reflect on its reason. Appreciate its intent. Think of its relevance. Promote its truth. Pass it on.

Enjoy with two glasses of white wine (of legal age), light a candle, draw a bath and relax.

Without further ado I present to you, *Gentlewoman.*

Introduction

Introduction: *The End*

The End.
Society is a broken mirror; but it's the only mirror she's got.
Her beauty convinced her she's ugly. Her mirror convinced her she's not.
Masculinity consumes her and power devours her.
Self-hate dates her and rapes her. Her womb is where the wounds were.
Scars worn by her successor.
Panties on the dresser.
Only pain can undress her.
Be careful how you address her.
Her decayed spirit is translucent.
There's no soul, but there's movement.
A corpse revived by lies. A mind destroyed by pollution.
She despises her body. She likes pies and lattes. She does Pilates.
She doesn't know what polite is.
Follows darkness like she doesn't know where the light is.
She's bright and knows what's wrong, but went left like she doesn't know what right is.
Her brain's caged like it's in the pen. She has no control like she's in Depends.
Has she lost her mind?
Well, it depends since ...
She's confused rebelliousness with independence.
Clever.
A sad girl mad at the change in weather.
A good girl gone bad, but not gone forever.
It's a bold, cold world–better grab a sweater.
Just know that after every storm, the weather gets better.

The tragic heroine destined for defeat.
What led to her demise? Did she retreat?
They say she's alive, but her spirit's deceased.
This is a book of war, but war always ends in peace.
The Beginning.

Spoiler Alert: You win

Lost Crown

Lost Crown: *Cold War*

Once upon a time – yeah, yeah, blah, blah.
This isn't your fairytale!
This is based on a true story…

Since the beginning of time, man has attempted to capture and convey the essence of a woman through works of art. Portions could be read in vivid descriptions of Eve. Da Vinci did his best. Shakespeare strived to scribble it. Pablo Picasso tried to paint it. Chuck Close came close. It's almost audible in the songs of Sinatra. Even the vulnerability in John Legend's vibrato exhausts every effort. Good try.

Well, I've thought of you for a long time–a long, long time. I've dreamed of your mind, your poise and your wit, your hair, your scent and your lips. Grammar wouldn't allow me to describe you. I sought you out and then I fell in love with you. This happened for consecutive summers; summers turned into seasons; seasons into decades. After 7,300 sunrises and sunsets, it came like an unexpected kiss from a bold crush. I got it! I'm prepared to introduce you.

The cursor blinks, but I don't. I've got red eyes on my red-eye. It's my 14th flight in 29 days–an average of one plane ride every other day. I've had great wine and a great time, but I'd rather be with you. I've witnessed every time zone on my iPhone and traveled a world full of pretty girls, but in my mind, all I saw was you.

You don't have a name anymore. Many reduce your humanity by calling you a female or a bitch, and far too many of you are answering the call. Fortunately many of you are interested in

28

acting like a Lady, but have been told to think like a man. Thinking like a man is a waste of a woman, but you should understand how men think. Men are behaving like women; women are behaving like men; and Ladies are getting lost in the mix. Your crown is up for grabs.

Have you ever seen a Lady? Not a woman, but a Lady. There's a difference. You're a girl by birth, a woman by maturity and a Lady by choice. Do you remember how the sight of a Lady made you feel? Did she smile at you? Could you feel her warmth? Do you remember her scent of comfort and truth? Can you recall how difficult it was explaining what you witnessed when she walked by? The sounds of her footsteps permeated halls like symphonies. Her high heels were music; her walk was a song. Watching her commanded an Oscar – she was a full-length motion picture. Was her facial structure not a piece of gorgeous architecture? Was her hair not a spilling waterfall? Was not even her blink the sunset and sunrise? The warm air…the cool breeze…the sound of waves crashing at the shore – was her whisper not like an evening at the beach? Was the sound of her voice not audible art with a melody that made you move? Did her mere presence not influence a nation? Is there any experience like experiencing her for the first time? Do you remember the first time you saw a Lady?

Well, when was the last time you saw her? She's a missing part of the conversation; an afterthought.

Like a torn condom, you've been left unprotected when needed most. You split because you felt neglected. Your Independence Day isn't July 4th, but every summer that passes, fireworks become less enjoyable in your absence. Trips to the beach are like walking past puddles because the ocean seems less significant in your absence. A sunset has been downgraded to a falling star without you. Beauty isn't beautiful anymore. Your uprooting has left open soil for rotten seeds. Bad girls sprout each spring. You've been bootlegged. Young girls are deceived by your knock-off. You're unreal. You're the tooth fairy and the Easter bunny, except kids don't even believe in you anymore. Your curtsy is gone. Your smile is vintage. There are remnants of your aura in classic films, while your ghost exists in love songs. Your name is an antique. Some say you can only be viewed in museums. Others say reality TV murdered you. Bad attitudes with skinny cigarettes have replaced you. People in costumes pretend to be you, but they're see-through. You're like black and white photography except you haven't made a comeback.

Has anyone seen a Lady?

Her being is being belittled, but her presence remains a present. She's gifted. The mere existence of a Lady controls attention, but too often the wrong attention. Most men give breast contact instead of eye contact when a Lady speaks. When women are placed on pedestals, some men will only look up to look up their skirts. Look up *"Lady"* in a thesaurus and you won't notice an ample supply of favorable synonyms. Most of what you'll see is simple or derogatory: *female; dame; broad; maid; damsel; wench*. Must I go on?

"Women are the most underused resource." **-Hillary Rodham Clinton**

Men in a group are commonly referred to as "gentlemen" regardless of their manners, but there's no equal term for women. God made us equal. Man made us unequal. Historically, we have

30

contributed greatly to your departure. The wars that were once waged over women are now being waged on women. Sometimes it's blatant and other times it's subtle. We want less competition in the workplace, so we've denied you equal pay. We've fired you for getting pregnant or demoted you when you returned from maternity leave. Many of us view you as second-class citizens. Deep down many of us hate you. We don't respect you. We view you as the weaker sex, and therefore, the unequal sex. We spit at your femininity. We curse your being. We've disenfranchised you. Many of us refuse to hold open doors unless you hold open legs. We'll toss you a twenty for a cab instead of driving you home and walking you up to your destination. We've blamed you for being victims of your own rape. We've blamed you for our infidelities. And now we are taking our blame on tour. Women have become a campaign issue. There's truly something deep-rooted about the state of men and women today. Any group that deliberately demoralizes and alienates its women is destructive. Why would we fight the very thing we desire? The very thing we need?

I myself have been guilty of friendly fire casualties. In an effort to progress you, I've sometimes failed you with patriarchal messages that seem to demote you from a place of equality. I'm sorry. I'd be a fool to say I have women all figured out. Women don't even have women figured out. But I've learned to rethink my approach and gain a deeper understanding of you. I've conducted thousands of tireless hours of research and go to battle in your favor. All I want to do is keep everyone alive. And contrary to patriarchal belief, the word "everyone" includes women.

"We are better off when women are empowered – it leads to a better society." **–John Legend**

Gentlewomen, we thirst for you. We want you. We need you back. Regardless of any negative behavior suggesting otherwise, we admire you. Forgive us for ignoring your strength and not acknowledging your greatness. Excuse us for acting like realtors and viewing you as property.

You're beyond brilliant. We take delight in your ability to progress, but we don't want to be replaced by big degrees and little dogs. I encourage you to turn this war on women into war for women. Fight for equal rights, equal pay and equal respect. We'll join you in battle. But refrain from fighting each other in the process. Don't fall for the rhetoric you're supposed to be at odds with each other. Stand united with your fellow Lady. And you don't have to hate us to be for the cause. Learn to love your fellow man and you can count on us to love you. It's not Venus versus Mars – it's Venus with Mars. You shouldn't have to live this beautiful life without us and we can't exist without you. It's not the way God intended it. We need each other to survive. Respecting each other is one of the first steps toward having a better world.

Furthermore, when has adversity kept a Lady down? It takes far more strength to maintain a gentle spirit amidst misfortune than it takes to surrender to anger. From the time a woman wakes up until the time she comes home, she deals with far more than most men would ever be able to properly handle. It fails to show on her face, but four persistent guys who think "no" means "yes" tried to talk to her on the way to work, and three more on her lunch break. Not to mention, she could've possibly dealt with a sexually inappropriate boss when she got there. A gentlewoman's toughness isn't expressed through a distressed forehead and a frown – it's intricately displayed via high heels, flats or sneakers on bruised toes, carrying the weight of humanity on her hips. Your resilience is brilliance. You're built to endure pregnancies, cramps and us. That doesn't just deserve a round of applause. That deserves a holiday!

Don't believe the great lie. You don't have to be Ladylike to command respect; you just have to be born. Your worth was determined the moment you were birthed. Your soul is legendary. A man's opinion alone should never change who you are – your own conviction should. Your own thirst for knowledge is the reason you're still turning these pages.

It's never too late to be a Lady.

Take your crown back.

"There is hope for that race or nation that respects its women."
-Sutton E. Griggs, *Imperium in Imperio*

Question the masculinity of a man threatened by a woman's femininity.

Kingdom Come

Kingdom Come: *Restoration*
They're deceived. They're calling wrong right and right wrong.

Mostly, they wanted to be loved. They wanted to be heard and understood. They wanted to be included and express their true selves without limitations. They wanted to matter. But you wouldn't let them. No! You restricted them and called them names. You tried to control them. They asked you to stop. They asked nicely, but you ignored it. They knocked on your doors, but you didn't answer. They cried out upon deaf ears. They filled up streets and city blocks and they marched until finally they said forget it! They snatched their rights and it was beautiful. They tasted freedom until their stomachs swelled. They consumed so much that they became drunk. Some were lawless. Others were lawyers. Some became a threat to the system that enslaved them. Others became a threat to themselves. A lot gained, but much lost. Lord, help us. Thy kingdom come, Thy will be done.

You can't put a Band-Aid on a tumor and expect it to go away. Society is sick. It's time to stop self-medicating and masking the pain with the wrong solutions. We can't keep disregarding societal issues hoping they'll just go away, or leave them up to someone else to fix. Quit saying it's not your problem. That's the problem. It is your problem. These issues are collectively our issues. If you don't take personal responsibility, then you can take personal blame. Regardless of class, race, sex or religion, we're all a part of the bigger picture. We're in this thing together.

We live in an era of reduced sensitivity. Some folks think thoughtfulness is something somewhere in their grandma's jewelry box. They think chivalry is some kind of fancy silverware.

Everyday we face unsettling humans with ill attitudes; a lack of manners, sense of entitlement and people who believe etiquette is irrelevant in this lifetime. Too many times, we react to life's confrontations negatively and end up missing the beauty in moments meant for us. Society is sick. *Gentlewoman* is half of the cure. The other half is up to you.

The truth won't hurt you—it'll heal you.

You're a Girl by birth, a Woman by maturity and a Lady by choice

Politeness is considered offensive. Some women call it degrading to have a door held open for them by a man. Simple smiles are seen as disingenuous. A compliment is desperation. They're calling chivalry *thirst* now.

CHIVALRY ≠ THIRST

THIRST /THərst/ noun: *A relentless and unhealthy desire of needing something or someone to the degree of embarrassment. Thirst has a detestable scent no perfume can mask and no shower can rinse. Thirst causes a dinner date to look like a rehearsal dinner. Thirst is unmistakable.*

Chivalry is the most basic form of respect. It's a gesture that's authentic and has no ulterior motives. It's a gesture that says, "I acknowledge your presence." It's a gesture that says, "I know three guys tried to talk to you on the way to work. I don't want your phone number. I just want to say good morning to brighten up your day." It's not overbearing. It doesn't expect anything. It should make you feel appreciated and valued. Chivalry comes from a pure and honest place and it desires nothing in return. You can say thank you.

YOUR MANNERS WILL REVEAL YOUR CHARACTER

Etiquette is a social contract that far too many violate and refuse to sign. While powerful women are busy running for president, men are frantically running from powerful women. The complex and often beautiful intricacies of a Lady are being devalued and degraded. It's tragic that a woman's femininity coupled with tenacity sparks confusion. Some men don't know how to accept nor deal with a woman's worth and prestige. You're called derogatory names in order to regulate your gender. It's an easy out. The use of colorful phrases helps the insecure to look past their shortcomings, inflating a deflated ego with a false sense of dominance and control. If it weren't for the tenacity of a woman, we would cease to exist. Women are the mothers of creation. How can man maneuver through life without the power of woman? A world minus the X chromosome is the death of mankind. We have to decrease the gap in gender and simply view each other as human beings.

Etiquette is an often misspelled, difficult-to-pronounce and intimidating word. It sounds like doves should fly and violins play every time you say it. Etiquette doesn't seem relatable. Popular culture suggests it's stuck in an era where only knights and queens dwell. Only the Buckingham Palace people still use it, right?

Wrong. Don't let high society fool you. Etiquette is the relief of your back on a New York subway because a gentleman gave up his seat for you to sit down. On a brisk day, etiquette is the comforting taste of a venti/nonfat milk/4-pump/sugar-free/skinny cinnamon dolce latte pre-purchased by the stranger at the front of the coffee shop line. It's lifting a burden from society by doing your part to contribute positively to it. Etiquette is simply polite behavior.

BE CAREFUL HOW YOU PORTRAY YOURSELF – OTHERS MIGHT BELIEVE YOU

This doesn't mean adjust your life for the world's convenience. You're not interested in simply being a people pleaser because you too, matter. Overly-caring what everyone thinks is the perfect way to live a meaningless life, but let's face it, not caring for yourself and others isn't living at all.

"Instead of putting others in their place, put yourself in their place."

-Amish Proverb

This philosophy is so vital that the best-selling book of all time commands us to love thy neighbor as thyself in Matthew 22:39. It's the golden rule: *One should treat others as one would treat oneself.* This same concept appears in the world's major religions including Hinduism, Buddhism and Islam. It's how several cultures resolve conflict. It's what the basis of *Gentlewoman* is about.

My wife made me revisit the golden rule when she caught me drinking lemonade from the container. "Now, if you caught me

drinking from the container, you'd be upset," she said. She was
right. It's a pet peeve of mine. My excuse was I did it because I
knew it wouldn't bother her. Is this a double standard? Maybe. But
it's not necessarily a bad double standard because she doesn't care
if I do it. It doesn't bother her. Let's revisit the golden rule of
treating people like we want to be treated. The reality is this rule
suggests everyone shares the same likes and dislikes. In reality,
things don't excite or bother everyone in the same manner. The
golden rule needs a bit of a tweak: Treat people *better* than you'd
like to be treated. This will ensure you treat them right despite your
biased personal preferences.

An added bonus is polite behavior has a reciprocal effect. Some
people call it karma. I call it the principle of reaping and sowing.
We're all walking seeds and what we say, do, think and how we
treat others is all coming back to us–all of it. When we take the
golden rule a step further and do unto others *better* than we would
have them do unto us, we create a space for reaping to be stored up
for stormy days.

Behave as if your parents raised you correctly... even if they didn't

The way you were raised is no longer an excuse. "Daddy wasn't
there, and mother tried her best" is no longer valid reasoning.
Eventually, there will be an external manifestation of an internal
problem. You're going to stumble, but the more you rely on an
unnecessary *crutch*, the more you forget that you can actually
walk. When does your story move beyond your excuse? When
does your test become your testimony? The only difference
between a successful and unsuccessful woman is one got back up.

A Lady should express her identity through her own point of view and not in relation to what men think about her. Human value isn't in the hands of people and worth is determined the moment one is born. However, it's important for a Lady to possess an awareness of how she's generally perceived. "Why is this important," you might ask? "How does this benefit me? Why should I care what some guy or anyone thinks about me, for that matter?"

Gentlewoman is worthy of you giving a damn because it contains insight from unbiased and outside minds, not because a man wrote it. Whether right or wrong, you will be thought of and remembered from the perspective of others. Your behavior is your billboard. You can be a phenomenal being, but if your behavior commonly suggests otherwise, the world will believe exactly what they see. People care about the opinions of the people they care about. If you maintain an "I don't give a damn" attitude, you potentially forfeit life connections that matter.

THE BAD NEWS IS THAT THE WORLD'S STANDARD OF RIGHT AND WRONG KEEPS CHANGING. THE GOOD NEWS IS THAT GOD'S STANDARD NEVER CHANGES.

What is a gentlewoman? Why would you want to be one? She's a contemporary Lady—one who adheres to a moral standard of living. She's well-dressed, well-spoken, well-traveled and well-read. And she's beautiful. It's OK to be beautiful. Accept it. Downplay it for no one. But understand what beauty is at its core. Beauty is the expression of your soul. Gentlewoman doesn't mean weak Lady. Her strength is in her cool demeanor. She's naturally cool, although it's no goal of hers to be. A gentlewoman is the Lady at an art show who discusses a mural with an admirer while not immediately giving away that she is the painter of the piece – she's humble. A gentlewoman is the Lady crossing the street turning heads with each stride – she's in vogue. A gentlewoman is seen on national news networks discussing complex and stimulating ideas one minute, and sitting courtside at an NBA game the next – she's balanced like that. A gentlewoman knows how to properly hold her wine glass by the stem, but doesn't give a damn if it spills – she's not perfect. You'd want to become her because a gentlewoman understands exactly who she is and makes no apology for it. She waits for the world to catch up.

DON'T BE INTIMIDATED BY HER – SHE IS YOU

In the meantime, we live in a time where just about anything is acceptable as long as you're keeping it real. You've got to be so slow if you think your ideas of being so real are keeping your soul real. When you compromise your integrity, morals and core values for the attention, admiration and false respect of others, it classifies you as phony. My heart bleeds and my soul aches for folks that do whatever it takes to keep it real when their soul is fake.

Sadly, on our quest to be a more open and accepting community, we've forgotten that society still has rules and not everything is acceptable. Not every action is OK and not every word in your head needs to be said. As our language has become coarsened, so has our behavior. In a lawless land, we must rebrand, re-establish and reintroduce the beautiful art of etiquette.

We start with each other. The problem isn't just that men don't like to court, it's that expectations have caused standards to drop. And most men I surveyed don't even know what courting is, let alone how to do it. Nowadays, showing a Lady interest means buying her a drink. And that drink might get us exactly what we want. That's the problem. The respect is gone and though you demand it, you don't always command it. You demand things with your words. You command them with your actions. For the most part, we will do what you allow. When a substitute teacher enters a classroom, the students size her/him up. If the substitute doesn't state intentions and expectations immediately, some students may intentionally misbehave. But if the substitute teacher commands that respect immediately, that's exactly what she/he gets. And if not, there are consequences. Therefore, the conclusion has been reached:

Society can't function without the presence of a Lady

You've come too far to turn back now. If you don't fit the description, don't turn the page.

The end of this page is the beginning of your return...

Pick up your crown.

"Woe to those who call evil good and good evil, who put darkness for light and light for darkness, who put bitter for sweet and sweet for bitter." –**Isaiah 5:20**

Interlude
Ten Commandments

Ten Commandments

- *Thou shalt not judge others by which thou do not possess thyself. If your only means of transportation are your Nikes, be ye not concerned with the model or make of a man's vehicle. Be not shallow if you don't have a pool.*
- *If you decide to be with a bad boy, you have no right to complain when he does bad boy things to you. Therefore I say, if a man is not macho enough for you, date a terrorist and let us know how that works out.*
- *Thou shalt cultivate diverse valuable friendships. For, if you are the smartest person in the room, you are indeed in the wrong room.*
- *Thou shalt manage expectations. If you wouldn't put a one dollar bill into a broken vending machine, why would you give your all to a man who never gives you anything in return? Art thou not worth more than one dollar and some Doritos? Possessing intellect serves no purpose if it is abandoned in moments that matter most. Why would thou throw away logic in relationships when thou value it in every other area of thy life? Common sense is thy heart's condom. Don't go unprotected.*
- *Thou shalt not offer the least and expect the most. I declare it is illegal to demand a man be six feet, make six figures and have a six-pack if you have bad feet, no figure and drink six packs. For I say unto you, until you meet your own checklist, please put the pen and paper down post-haste.*
- . *Thou shalt not pretend to be a single man's wife. Thy boyfriend is not thy husband. Giving marriage privileges to a boyfriend is like giving an intern the CEO's salary. Thou art paying full price for partial service.*
- *Thou shalt not chase. When you chase a man, he is running from you. Eat that truth and swallow the reality. If thirsty, help thyself to a glass of dignity. Bon appétit.*

- *Thou shalt not say all men are the same – thou shalt say thou date the same type of men. To suggest all men are the same is to suggest God lacks creativity.*
- *Thou shalt pay attention. Intellect is free, but ignorance will cost you.*
- *Thou shalt not search elsewhere for what already exists within. The first greatest love thou will find is God. The second greatest love thou will find is in the mirror. Enjoy the view.*

Pleasantries

Pleasantries: *Gentlewoman's Law*

Rules, rules, rules! Haven't you had enough? Can't you just be left alone and live the life you want to live? Of course, but keep my mantra in mind:

*Disobeying life's **little** rule can result in **big** consequences.*

"Only God can judge me" is no longer an excuse for bad behavior

They say only rebels reject rules, but many old rules need to be broken. Unfortunately, society is pushing the limit with how many rules it can shatter. Fortunately, not all broken laws warrant arrest.

Self-expression is a beautiful freedom and shouldn't be regulated as long as it's not invading another's personal space. But don't *overdose* on freedom. Not every action is OK. Sometimes you affect others negatively and freedom won't justify your behavior. Yes, you're free to walk around with offensive breath, but you shouldn't. Mints are free in glass bowls at every front desk in a restaurant near you. Look next to the toothpicks.

While we have established the need for gentlewomen in our culture, the practices of the well-mannered Lady are firmly rooted in comfortable and natural behavior. If at anytime it doesn't feel right, you're not doing it right. Open up this book, turn to this section and try again.

In this chapter, we will examine codes of conduct for your consideration and most of all, for you to apply and repeat with confidence and ease. These rules aren't put in place to blindly obey. Think about each rule and how it applies to your life or the lives of others. Use these tools to rebuild what's broken and build upon what's already beautiful. The unwritten laws of the society of gentlewomen are as follows:

Rule n° 1 *A woman who knows her worth is a damn powerful woman*. Figure it out.

Rule n° 3 *Kindness*: It can turn a frown upside-down, an attempted suicide to life and a hater to a lover. Plus, it's free! It might cost you your ego, but you should've thrown that away when you picked up this book. Being friendly, generous and considerate is underrated. Regardless of your position in life, your accolades or you wealth, how you treat people is what they'll remember. Joseph Joubert said, "A part of kindness consists in loving people more than they deserve." There will be countless opportunities for you to be rude, but instead be kind. This shows you're in control of your emotions.

BE KIND TO PEOPLE. YOU NEVER KNOW WHOM YOU'RE TALKING TO.

There have been many times I've treated strangers kindly and didn't have to. It just so happens that I've run into many of those same strangers later in life and the tables were turned. They were now in the position to help me out. That's how life works! Be warmhearted, show compassion and gentleness, but don't let your kindness be taken for weakness. Stand up for any injustice. Just don't treat others with that same injustice. Be kind to all, even

49

those ugly on the inside. They're likely going through pain that has
nothing to do with you.

ACTING NICE IS DECEPTIVE. BEING NICE IS BEAUTIFUL. BE BEAUTIFUL.

Random Acts of Kindness: Have you ever reached for your purse to
pay a bridge toll, only for the toll collector to tell you the debt has
already been paid? No? OK, have you waited in line at a Starbucks
to get your typical morning tall, half skinny/half 1 percent extra
hot, two shots decaf /two shots regular latte with extra whip, but
the stranger ahead ordered it for you already? And paid? Not
likely. It doesn't seem to cross the average mind to look out for a
neighbor. If we don't know them, we don't owe them.
It seems most people don't *really* care about anyone outside of
their immediate family and friends. If it's a good day, you might
toss a persistent panhandler with a creative cardboard some
crumpled cash, but that's about it. Selfishness is an interesting
concept because the way we treat others is, in fact, the way we are
treating ourselves. How? Well, everything comes back full circle
and what we put out eventually comes back to us–all of it. Yes,
even that very thing you just thought up that you thought you were
in the clear for. Hopefully this prompts you to do for people better
than you would like them to do for you. You're really doing for
you when you do for them after all!

GOOD THINGS COME TO THOSE WHO DO WELL

Giving gets bad PR. People cling onto their possessions and ideas.
Death is a friendly reminder that we don't truly own anything.
Don't you know you can't have good relationships unless you're
giving? You can't properly raise children unless you're giving.

You can't work a job unless you're giving. The world operates on the basis of giving. You get what you give. Selflessness doesn't sound so bad after all, does it? What costs you the least generally produces the greatest benefit. A small compliment can save a life. A short prayer can save a soul. Random acts of kindness are uncommon in progressive society. Buying someone a drink should come without expectations.

"Remember there's no such thing as a small act of kindness. Every act creates a ripple with no logical end." –**Scott Adams**

Let's have some fun. I challenge you to pay it forward. Do something greater than you for someone other than you. It's not everyone's job to stay out of your way; it's your job to react in love. It took me three years to deliver this book to you. The least you can do is pay for the complicated latte of the next person in line at Starbucks. Extra whip, please!

"Above all, love each other deeply, because love covers over a multitude of sins."
-1 Peter 4:8

Rule n° 5 *Chivalry is for Ladies, too*: Chivalry is a term often debated and sometimes hated with a meaning no one seems to agree upon. Historically, chivalry originated between the 11th and 15th centuries as a knight's moral code to protect those who couldn't protect themselves (children, elders and widows). The definition has since dropped its original intent and simply means the respect and honor of women. However, there are some women who view chivalry as an insult. When looking at its original definition coupled with its current meaning, it might seem that chivalry is indeed suggesting women are helpless and dependent on men. And that's where the problem lies. Chivalry was originally intended for babies, kids, old people and women whose husbands had died. During this time period, most husbands were the sole providers for their families and if they perished, assistance was needed. People are mixing one part of an old definition with another part of the current one. We know women are capable of the same life skills as men. Chivalry isn't about male dominance. In the 21st century, chivalry should just mean honoring the opposite sex. In relationships, chivalry shows a mutual respect for your partner. In everyday life, chivalry strengthens men and women's relations. Whether or not you believe in gender roles, they shouldn't shape social norms around courteous behaviors. Holding open doors today is more about courtesy and less about helping the defenseless. Courteous behavior isn't limited to men. Chivalry is for Ladies, too.

Here are eight easy ways a Lady can be chivalrous:

- **Massages after a long day is chivalrous.**
- **After we open your car door and let you in, lean over and push the driver's side door open. It's a literal thank you, a reciprocating gesture that shows equal respect. That's good chivalry.**
- **If you're on the driver's side and we pump your gas, wait until we walk around to the passenger's side of the car before you start the engine so the exhaust fumes don't get all over us. That's chivalrous.**
- **When it's cold and we offer you our jacket, offer us your scarf or a hug to keep us warm. Very chivalrous.**

- o Calling to see if you can pick up anything to eat on the way home after we've had a long day is a display of chivalry.
- o If he's been a great partner in the relationship, take him out on a date and attempt to pay. That's chivalrous.
- o Offering to do the dishes after we've cooked is an awesome sign of chivalry.
- o If a stranger is struggling for the door, prop it open. Man or woman. Get the point?

"CHIVALRY IN PUBLIC MEANS NOTHING WHEN THERE'S A LACK OF RESPECT IN PRIVATE." –SAMANTHA LUCK

Chivalry isn't for applause, but when someone displays an honorable gesture toward another, a signal of appreciation is warranted. Though it's not required, a simple "thank you" is common practice. If you believe the golden rule is to treat others *better* than you want to be treated, you can take it a step further by reciprocating with a kinder action.

There are many things expected of us as gentlemen and we work hard to provide. We're not looking for praise, just don't underestimate the value of a thank you or reciprocated gesture. Paraphrased, Galatians 6:7 says, "A (wo)man reaps what (s)he sows." Therefore, if you require chivalry, then be chivalrous.

Chivalry isn't intended to demean. Chivalry is a display of love intended to display admiration and faith in humankind. We understand you can hold open your own door, but we hold open doors because we love you. It's completely natural for a man to want to protect those he loves.

Feminism is about equality. Equality is about being able to make a choice. Being a Lady of choice means you get to make one. Whether a gentlewoman chooses to have a career or stay at home with the kids, she's the one who makes that decision. A contemporary gentlewoman proud of the inability to cook or clean is ridiculous. Being domestic isn't a duty, but not knowing how to take care of yourself or others is a disgrace. If you don't care to be domestic, that's your choice. If another Lady loves being domestic, that's her choice. The same women who fought for her to have a choice should never critique her about her decisions. Sometimes the main people setting you back can be your own.

Chivalry is simply courteous behavior. Historically it has been courteous behavior specifically geared toward women. But with huge advances in the social standing of women over the years, equal treatment is commonplace. Gentlemen deserve to be treated chivalrously by Ladies, too. Chivalry involves courting, but extends beyond the boundaries of dating. Chivalry is a way of life. It shows a world that doesn't give a damn that you do!

You don't have to agree. As long as the conversation is created and the people are talking, my job here is done.

Rule n° 7 *A successful Lady who wants a successful man isn't a gold-digger–she's smart.* Ironically, those most concerned about gold-diggers have no gold to be dug! The reality is not every woman who wants a fancy meal is a gold-digger, and not every man who refuses to fund that meal is broke. The real issue is if you love him for who he is despite what he has at the moment. We all deserve what we offer and have the *real* potential to offer.

Rule n° 9 *You can't judge a man by his shoes – billionaire Steve Jobs wore New Balances and Jesus wore sandals.* If Mr. Right is right in front of you, you probably missed him because he has on the wrong shoes. It's all about perspective and at a certain point you must realize what's truly important. Classic gangsters wore suits…you can't judge a man by what he wears. We're born naked. Fashion is just life's cool accessory. Don't get too caught up in the hype.

NOTE: The urban sophisticate consumes goods that are subtle and not necessarily recognizable by the general public, but by those in the know. His possessions may not always look it, but they cost much more than the flashy man's bright suit and flashy shoes. Contemporary gentlemen prefer private pleasures to public swagger and keep their personal portfolio privileged. Sorry.

Rule n° 11 *When you make us work, the boys will fade and the gentleman will remain.* A Lady hardest to get is the easiest to keep because working hard for something makes us appreciate it that much more. This isn't about giving us an unnecessary hard time for your ego to be stroked. It's about insisting that we put real efforts in our pursuit. Being hard to get has more to do with you fully understanding your worth and refusing to settle, and less to do with some game you're playing. Be hard to get, don't play it. And when we earn you, honor us. We'll forever honor you.

Rule n° 13 *Managed entitlements*: Your existence doesn't mean you're owed anything except love, life and the pursuit of happiness. Anything extra is earned. You're entitled to what you struggle for. Stop expecting anyone to do for you what you're unwilling to do for yourself. Yes, you're God's gift to the world, but so are seven billion others.

Rule n° 15 *Texting isn't courting*. Everyday text messaging isn't a real relationship…you two are just pen pals. People need affection. People need feeling. People need hugs. People need people in real life. Let's get back to basics, people.

Rule n° 17 *Non-violence*: A Lady isn't interested in violence. It's OK to admit hurt. It's not OK to retaliate. Resolve that pain instead of acting on it. You're allowed to be upset about injustice. Go ahead and be angry. You do well to be angry—but don't use your anger as fuel for revenge. And don't stay angry. Don't go to bed angry. Don't give evil that kind of foothold in your life. What's the point in beating the bullies if you just take their place?

Rule n° 19 *Don't be with him unless you'd be proud to have a son exactly like him*. And while you're at it, be the woman you'd want your daughter to be and the Lady you'd want your son to date.

Rule n° 21 *Consideration*: Thoughtfulness and sensitivity for others is the basis of what being a gentlewoman is all about. It's not always all about you. If you order to-go food over the phone and something comes up, call to cancel the order. You'd be surprised at how many people don't execute that simple gesture. If you work in customer service, always consider your customer and always give great service. This sounds like common sense, but common sense is uncommon. Don't bring crying babies to rated R movies. If you take out a pack of gum in front of others, offer them a piece. If you're not in a sharing mood, wait until you're alone to take it out, or fake a yawn to put it in your mouth. Put yourself in other's shoes.

Rule n° 23 *In a closet full of clothes, you say you have nothing to wear – be that selective in a room full of men*. A single Lady who doesn't make men her primary focus will always have options – A single Lady who *thirsts* for men will always be single. Men generally focus on women who focus on themselves. You don't chase love–you attract it. It's given freely. You don't have to beg or sell your soul for it. You just have to accept it.
NOTE: You may feel like you offer a lot, but don't have many options. You will always have options. Whether or not you like those options is an entirely different story. You should never change your core standards, just your idea of what we think the manifestation of those standards look like.

Rule n° 25 *Politeness*: It's easy to be polite in the company of politeness. The real challenge is maintaining politeness in the company of an ass. Your mood should never dictate your manners.

Rule n° 27 *Don't believe the hype that your standards are too high because you desire what you offer*. Never allow people with no goals and no ambition to convince you of this. Too many women without pets go home to dogs. Release the leash. If he complains about meeting your basic standards and can't notice a good woman in front of him, perhaps he'll notice when you're gone. You deserve a gentleman.
NOTE: Some women *do* have unrealistic standards. They face a world where those standards aren't met, so they settle and assume there aren't any good men based on results from searching under impractical pretenses. Don't be her.

Rule n° 29 *Integrity*: A gentlewoman of integrity has a strong moral uprightness. She doesn't allow anyone or anything to compromise her core. Man can't control her morals and money won't sway her. Money can be replaced, but integrity can't.

Rule n° 31 *Never stop flirting with him, even if he's yours*. The occasional inappropriate activity at an inappropriate place and an inappropriate time is completely appropriate. Don't be so classy that you're not a little nasty.

Rule n° 33 *Nonjudgmental*: The world is broken and incomplete along with the people in it. No one has arrived. No one is better than anyone else. No one is perfect. Nothing is guaranteed. We're all out here trying to make it. Pointing your finger at others results in three of your own fingers pointing back at you. It's a friendly reminder to judge you before you judge them.

It's a tragic world we live in when extortionists hate rapists and adulterers shun liars. They're all one in the same. And if it weren't for grace, we'd all be judged the same. Matthew 7:3 says, "Why do you look at the speck of sawdust in your brother's eye and pay no attention to the plank in your own eye?" When you make mistakes you suffer the consequence and eventually move on, so why won't you provide that same grace to others? It's irresponsible to believe your own hype. You have skeletons in your closet, too. The only difference between you and those you judge is your ability to deceive people into thinking you're perfect. You can learn something from those you condemn.

Don't judge someone else because they sin differently than you. No sin is greater or lesser in the eyes of God.

Rule n° 35 *Privacy*: What is it that drives people to inquire about the personal affairs of others when it serves them no benefit? Is it an innate curiosity, or a more trivial matter of gossip that drives folks to unnecessarily involve themselves in business that isn't theirs? Perhaps it's a selfish desire for attention that provokes some to willingly give up all that's sacred.

"When made public, love rarely endures." -Andreas Capellanus

Translated today, the statement above simply means, if you let the world in your relationship, the world will end your relationship. This form of discretion doesn't mean keep your love life hidden in the dark – you're supposed to let your light shine. It means be wise about the information you share and with whom you share it with.

Transparency serves its purpose when it benefits the lives of others. If it doesn't, then it isn't their business. On the other hand, being opaque is obscure and impenetrable, but allows no light in. So live translucently. A translucent life permits a percentage of light to pass through depending on several variables, but isn't clearly see-through. In other words, living translucently lets you control who has access to your life depending on your level of trust for them. Live a translucent life.

Consistent bragging about how good your man is in bed might cause your "girlfriends" to try to find out for themselves. Learn to keep certain aspects of intimacy and your love life private.

"A beautiful woman who lacks discretion is like a gold ring in a pig's snout." **–Proverbs 11:22**

Rule n° 37 *Morals*: These are a gentlewoman's principles of right and wrong behavior. Morals define one's character. It's where the very thread of the cloth from which you're cut is woven. Put great thought into what you stand for and let your morals guide you. Never compromise them and never lose your values. When you forfeit your morals, you forfeit your soul. There's plenty of room to mess up, but always get back to virtue. Reflect on the woman you want to be and the legacy you want to leave.

Rule n° 39 *Happiness*: It's a choice. Happy people have mastered the art of happiness by controlling the way they respond to what life throws at them. The quicker you figure this out, the sooner you'll enjoy life. Oh, and if everyone's happy with you, you're doing something wrong.

Rule n° 41 *Compliments*: Compliments are vintage. Not that cool vintage that commands the respect of those both young and old, but that prehistoric vintage that smells old and seems outdated. Props to those who give props to those who deserve props, because far too many treat compliments like a kiss by someone with aggressive breath – hard to give.

It's necessary to acknowledge the greatness in others because flattery humbles both the giver and the receiver. Giving a compliment is simply stating the obvious with an expression of admiration. Admiration is part of the human spirit. We're supposed to feel good when others look good and do well. A compliment can turn a bad time into the perfect moment. It can even save the life of someone reconsidering living. When we think of it like that, maybe we'll be more generous giving others what they truly deserve – love.

However, there is such a thing as overdoing it. Too many compliments can be an annoyance. Telling someone how great he or she looks five times in five minutes is aggressive and weird. Some compliments are inappropriate. Don't compliment a young Lady for appearing older than she looks. And don't compliment another Lady's beau more than once. Use discernment.

Rule n° 43 *If you don't go on dates with the person you date, then you're not dating.* Pretty simple, huh?

Rule n° 45 *Humility:* Stay humble. Loud arrogance is quiet insecurity. *Sexy* hardly speaks and *greatness* doesn't have to say it's great. So walk gently leaving heavy footprints. Vanity is simply foundation and concealer for the self-conscious. But we see right through you.

Having humility doesn't mean you shouldn't be your best, look your best and do your best. Just keep it Bercolaesque!

Rule n° 47 *If you think being single sucks, it's because you do.* When you can't stand your own company, no one else will either. Fall in love with you first.

Rule n° 49 *Honesty:* Everything that no one is saying needs to be said. There's a thin line between tact and tolerance. There's too much hypersensitivity and political correctness. A gentlewoman believes in acceptance, but she also believes in correction. She believes in tolerance, but she also believes in accountability. Not everyone is "hating" on you–someone is telling you the truth. And the truth changes things. Not every word spoken requires an apology.

TRUTH WILL ALWAYS TRUMP WHAT YOU "THINK"

Honesty is a foreign language. Not many can speak it and hardly anyone understands it. A "friend" who doesn't inform you of your ill behaviors is an enemy who doesn't want to see you prosper. Speak truth now and hand out Band-Aids later. Growth isn't always comfortable. You'll grow weary running from the truth. Everything that's in the dark must eventually come to the light.

Rule n° 51 *Character*: Built from difficult and sometimes unpopular decision. Beneath any façade, this is truly who you are. You may give the world your alter ego, but your character will sleep with you at night and wake with you in the morning. It never leaves. It will still exist when you're dead and gone. You can't get rid of it, but you can change it.

Rule n° 53 *Selflessness*: The true measure of selflessness is helping someone who can't return the favor.

Rule n° 55 *You can change the world faster than you can change a man*. Some women will compromise with the idea that they can change a man down the line. Unless he's in diapers, you won't be changing him. You can't raise an adult. You are guaranteed to always fail. Stop trying. Date what is; not what you hope will be. You'll know it when you see it. You can't change your man, but you can change your mind.
Quit holding yourself responsible for an adult. Learn how to change a tire – Forget about changing a man.
NOTE: When you focus on adding to us instead of changing us, we'll want to change for you.

Rule n° 57 *Punctuality***:** One of the most disrespectful acts you can commit is to have no regard for someone else's time. It's a lazy gesture that says: I value other things more than you. Set all your clocks fast to trick yourself into thinking it's later than it is. You can plan ahead by preparing directions the evening before. Get ready in the mornings even if you don't have plans. You never know what might come up. If you stay ready, you won't have to get ready.

Just don't underestimate the power of time. When you think you have enough, it'll pass you by in an instant. Don't give into the illusion of idle time. Checking text messages, browsing the Internet, wrapping up work, etc. will eat up the clock. Always give yourself an extra 30-minute window at least.

Unforeseen events can happen beyond your control causing you to be late. In this case, have the courtesy to call the person(s) waiting on you and give them a new estimated time of arrival.

Being late isn't the end of the world. Never put yourself or anyone else in danger just to be on time. That means no speeding to get there. It's better to arrive late than dead.

Rule n° 59 *Positive Element of Surprise:* When you under-promise and over-deliver, you foster grounds for loyalty. Giving people better than what they expect is a good thing! It generally keeps them coming back for more. Apply this principle wherever it helps.

Rule n° 61 *Common Sense***:** Assuming everyone knows about common sense suggests you have none. It's a valuable commodity that's free. You're born with it. You either listen to it, or you don't. If everyone knew how to use it, I'd be out of business.

NOTE: The only way to know what someone is thinking is to have a conversation about it...with them.

Rule n° 63 *When a grown man is interested – there's no guessing game or fishing for answers...there's no damn doubt about it.* Live life and stop boggling your mind. If a confident man wants you, he'll make the necessary moves to address you. If he doesn't, he's not serious or is uninterested. Get on with life.

Rule n° 65 *Control Personal Habits in Public:* That weird sound you make to scratch your throat; picking of the nose, spitting and even foul language should be limited in public places. The world isn't your living room. Remember, good etiquette is rooted in consideration for your neighbor(s).

Rule n° 67 *Pet Control:* There's a dog in my neighborhood whose owner thinks our lawn is a toilet. If I ever catch them two in action...well, let's just say, they wouldn't like it if I walked in their living room, grabbed a newspaper and helped myself to a bowel movement on their carpet. Sounds disgusting, right?

Pet owners...control your pets! You must respect the personal space of non-pet owners. Not everyone thinks it's cute when Dodo the dog does the deed.

Rule n° 69 *Love Excessively:* The world needs what you've got. Please don't withhold your supply due to a few rotten people. Love is best displayed when given to those who don't deserve it. Love is always worth it. The people who need the most love will ask for it in the most unloving ways. Never allow other's discourtesy, rudeness or bad attitudes to change the core of who you are. You're responsible for your reaction to others. Love over everything. Don't be naïve, but do be love. Love hard. Love passionately. Love always.

NOTE: Love people and use things. Don't use people and love things. But you knew that already.

Rule n° 71 *Dealing with Racism:* It's ignorant to believe we live in a post-racial society. Some people think race is only an issue if one makes it an issue. They think talking about something that creates division creates more division, or ignoring racism makes it go away. I wonder if ignoring cancer has that same effect.

The issue with pointing out racism is that it's not always black and white. Sometimes it's overt, other times it's covert. It's not always easy to prove, but it's there. A gentlewoman stands for justice and always stands her ground. But be aware of any threats and pay attention to your surroundings. If you ever experience something beyond your jurisdiction, notify the proper authorities. Just don't go putting the law in your own hands.

Rule n° 73 *Cooking:* Cooking can be viewed as a belittling domestic duty in the minds of some women. The thought of dishes, poultry and mitts might make some men over the moon and some women mince out of the room!

Cooking isn't a duty. Cooking is an action of affection. When my father cooks, he always says, "This was made with love." And we all can taste it, too! Eating is a necessity and someone has to cook the food. Sometimes it'll be a man. Sometimes it'll be a woman. Don't look too deeply into it. The decision to prepare and throw food in an oven doesn't make you any more or less of a woman. It doesn't have to be *your thing*. Let's hope you know how to make yourself a sandwich.

NOTE: Many men love to eat well and therefore love a Lady who can cook well. Many women also love to eat good food and love a man who knows how to put meat in the oven –unless you're vegan, then maybe he'll eat out.

Rule n° 75 *Know the difference between loyalty and stupidity.*
Too many women dic a spiritual, emotional and even physical death in the name of *loyalty*. A lot of "ride or die chicks" are dead. Why are you expected to be strong, faithful and reliable to a broken man who's the exact opposite to you? Being supportive is admirable, but be supportive with discernment and boundaries– especially if you're just dating. Being *loyal* to a man generally doesn't involve putting your life, family or destiny in danger. While *holding* your man down, don't hold your future down in the process. Be loyal to your purpose. Be loyal to your God. Be loyal to yourself. There's a thin line between being down for a man and being dumb for a man…watch your step!

To be "ride or die" is to have blind obedience. To truly be loyal is to be one of our biggest supporters when the world is against us, but set us straight when we're wrong.

Rule n° 77 *Handshakes:* Brief, but firm is best for the professional arena. It shouldn't hurt you, but it should wake you up. Give good eye contact and exchange momentary pleasantries. In more personal settings, this may be omitted altogether.

Rule n° 79 *Make us miss you sometimes.* Don't go overboard, but when executed with precision, there's power in this. Trust me.

Rule n° 81 *Be careful - a**holes wear suits, too.* Don't be fooled into thinking well-tailored clothes make him a gentleman. Classic gangsters wore classic suits well, as well.

Rule n° 83 *Date people, not potential.* If his potential doesn't lead to his progress, then you're just dating an idea. Don't let potential blind you into thinking who he could be is who he is. Too many women are dating men with expired potential. If you're succeeding in life and supporting him, and he's forever and always *about to* do something, but never once has he done anything, it's time to dispose of that unequal yoke. What good is a seed that has the potential to grow, but remains a seed? Undeveloped, undiscovered and misused gifts dishonor the Creator. Our gifts are His investments in us and He deserves His return. But so do you!

Rule n° 85 *Be Hospitable:* Always say, "Thank you." It's a simple sign of gratitude and praise. Don't forget, "You're welcome," "Excuse me," "Please," "Hello" and "Goodbye." Don't ask, "How are you?" if you don't want to know – only exchange genuine pleasantries.

Rule n° 87 *Don't Whisper in the Company of Others:* Secrets seem sinister and make the person who can't hear feel isolated. Just text it!

Rule n° 89 *Art of the Apology:* In a polite society, an apology is a useful tool and welcome gift. As an act of remorse for a mistake or misstatement, an apology is a sign of concern, respect and cultured behavior. There are, however, people who misuse apologies or employ apologies as a substitute for other behaviors. Simply put, these misuses are signs of immature or rude behavior. It's important to beware and be wary of the apology. Here are the guidelines for apologies:

Only When Appropriate

Apologies are useful when a mistake or accident has occurred: stepping on someone's toes, inadvertently cutting in line, dropping a cup, etc. The apology should be heartfelt, clear and direct. You may offer two thoughts of the following suggestion (but never three):

- o *I'm so sorry*
- o *Will you please excuse/forgive me*
- o *I apologize for the error*

Turn to face the sufferer(s) of the accident and speak directly to them. An apology offered with your back to the person, or tossed off while you are walking away, is not an actual apology and can be interpreted as an insult.

Be Specific

Though it may lead to a fight, *"Forgive me for taking your man"* is preferable to *"Hey, sorry."*
And while she's delighting in taking your man, go ahead and give her your shoes, too–she'll be walking in them. It's been said that if a woman *steals* your man, there's no better revenge than letting her keep him.

Do Not Apologize When an Apology is Not Called For

Some people use an apology when they actually want to say something else. For example, if you cannot hear someone, you should say, *"Excuse me?"* not *"I'm sorry?"* An apology is a statement, not a question.

The Apology Should Fit the Gaffe

If you've called someone who is hard to look at, ugly—apologize once—quickly—and get on with life. If a man is physically unattractive, don't refer to him as ugly–say, "He has a great personality." If you've wrecked a friend's car, the apology should be more substantial. In addition to offering to fix the vehicle, you might consider a note of regret and perhaps a free car wash. It's important to align the apology with the magnitude of the gaffe.

The Apology Should Not Be More Substantial than the Gaffe

While it's important to make amends, overly effusive, demonstrative and/or extravagant apologies will make the sufferer feel even worse. The victim of the gaffe will resent your effusiveness, suspecting that the apology was intended to relieve your guilt rather than to make them feel better. Remember, an apology is for the other person, not for you. *Empathy diminishes the distance between the accused and the victim.*

For Small or Medium Blunders, *Apologize Once*

A mistake is a mistake. One mistake gets one apology. If you apologize repeatedly for a single mistake, the sufferer will construe that you are insincere or worse. No need to apologize endlessly over a minor infraction. You'll be, in the vernacular, a pain in the ass. You're not really apologizing as much as you're going through some sort of insecure psychological episode. Go away!

An Apology Is a Bridge, Not a Destination

In polite behavior, an apology allows you to rise above an error, mistake or blunder. Once you've crossed that bridge, put it behind you and the sufferer. Don't wallow in the moment any longer than comfort and decorum permits. It's over.

Rule n° 91 *Forgiveness*: Death probably feels better than betrayal. The sharp sensation of having your heart seized, torn and discarded is one of the most severe of human emotions. At least when you die, there's no residual feeling of death. It's just poof and you're gone! But when you're emotionally beaten to a bloody pulp while conscious, forgiveness sounds like a foreign language.

Let's not confuse things – forgiveness doesn't restore trust, but it's an opportunity to rebuild it. It's not about wiping away consequences; it's about creating possibilities. We were created to love. What's the purpose of a heart if it doesn't love? What's the purpose of a life without a heart? Sometimes you have to accept apologies you never received. Forgive without residual anger.

Many of you are more forgiving than we are. But sometimes the most difficult person to forgive is you. God has already forgiven you – it's about time you do the same for yourself.

Rule n° 93 *Business and Pleasure*: Climbing the ranks in business doesn't require climbing into a man's pants. You don't have to make your neck hurt to network. You get to the top with your mind, not your mouth!

Rule n° 95 *Learn something new every three months:* Challenge yourself to get beyond yourself. When you make a commitment to growth, your life will feel enriched in areas unimagined.

Rule n° 97 *Pray:* It changes the things that people can't change.

Rule n° 99 *Eat alone***:** Life isn't about waiting for moments to happen. You don't have to wait on a date to eat or wait on marriage to start living. Catch a decent movie, a good meal and some nice wine–alone. A woman who knows how to enjoy her own company is an attractive woman. Sometimes you have to get your own flowers. Never wait on anyone else to love you before you do

Rule n° 101 *Forget the rules*. Sometimes some rules must be broken. If you've found someone who loves you like crazy and you love that person like crazy, be crazy in love. Make it work!

Tact: "*It is tact that is golden, not silence.*" **-Samuel Butler** Tact is the art of knowing when to shut up. It's an art. It's a calculated awareness and sensitivity to others and your environment. People without tact have bad taste. They justify tactlessness with *keeping it real*. Keeping it real is respected, but having tact is admirable. Tell the truth in a way that doesn't set out to offend. Tact is placing "Pleasantries" at the end of a harsh statement to soften the blow. Keep it classy or keep it to yourself.

Tipping Tips: If you can afford to enjoy life's little luxuries, you can afford to tip. Knowing whom to tip and how much can be an issue. Think of it like this: People who do services for you that you're capable of doing yourself likely fit the description of who you should give gratuity to. Here a just a few examples:

- **Hairstylist:** 20 percent is average. In the past, salon owners refused customer tips. But today, owners who provide services should be tipped. However, the owner may refuse tips out of consideration for employees who make a lower salary. If bunches of people are working on your hair, they might all expect gratuity. Let the owner know your preference before arrival so you're not penny-pinched.
- **Spa/Massage Therapist:** 15-20 percent.
- **Pet Groomer:** 15-20 percent for appreciation, 30 percent if they went the extra mile, or simply whatever you can afford.
- **Restaurant Servers:** 15-20 percent depending on the style of restaurant (tip may already be included at high end venues – you're not obligated to add extra, but if the service is outstanding, feel free).
- **Bartender:** 10-15 percent of total tab.
- **Bottle/Table Service at Nightclub:** 20 percent is standard (usually already included).
- **Doorman/Concierge:** $5-$20 is customary. Anything more is extra.
- **Car Service/Taxi:** 15-20 percent and then round up
- **Valet:** 20 percent of parking fee for good service; a bit more for great service. If valet is free, feel free to tip more.

Even if the service isn't phenomenal, tip something anyway. Sometimes tips are split among the staff. Take all into consideration.

What was once a sign of gratitude has become an expectation. If you're on the receiving end of a tip, show appreciation. Tips should be earned, not expected. Don't catch an attitude for receiving less than you feel you deserve. Work diligently in all you do–if not for tips, for your own character. Whatever you do, work at it with all your heart to honor the One who created you. **NOTE:** Special care must be taken to ensure that your well-meaning gesture isn't seen as insulting. I once enjoyed a glass of wine in Milan, Italy. The pizza was like sex. I attempted to leave my server a tip, but she profusely refused. Tipping just isn't suggested in certain cultures. Do your homework. Know what's customary wherever you travel. Observe the locals, and follow their lead.

Laughing Etiquette: Doesn't this just sound ridiculous. Traditionally, a Lady is taught to place two fingers over her closed mouth while she laughs. But laughing is a display of your soul. It's an uncontrollable symbol of happiness that can't be contained by two dainty fingers. Go ahead and laugh. Let your soul breathe. To laugh is to live. Do, however, try your best to refrain from falling out, snorting and/or causing a scene, but if you do, so what. You're still a gentlewoman!

Text Etiquette: **Most women like it orally.** The best way to misunderstand someone is through text messaging because the greatest miscommunication occurs over keyboards. Not to mention, smartphone autocorrect is dumb. Texting is a simplified method of communication intended for short phrases and quick communication. If your text message reads like a novel, pick up the phone and call.

The long-term effects of texting are yet to be determined, but the short-term effects are ever-present. A generation of texters is becoming accustomed to impersonal communication. The ramifications are seen in a lack of social skills–no eye contact, lack of discussion topics and the inability to connect.

It's far too obvious to state that texting while driving is dangerous, but what about texting while dating? Society seems satisfied with quick and convenient conversations. Relationships are a state of connectedness between people. Remember when the two of you would fight about who would hang up the phone first? Or how about when he mustered up the courage to ask you for your phone number, you wrote it down on the palm of his hand and you couldn't wait for him to call? Technology is taking the life out of relationships. People need human interaction to survive. Pressing buttons to get a date takes effort out of the courting process. If we don't work for it, we won't respect it. Dating by text is completely unacceptable other than, "I'm on the way," "Running a little late," "Red wine or white," etc. Pick up the phone and say her name. She's a grown woman. Teens text–adults talk. Someone who text messages you 100 percent of the time is often a sign of someone who isn't 100 percent interested in you. To build relationships on text is to build a bridge on ice–the foundation isn't strong enough to sustain when the heat is on.

Aren't you tired of settling for being "texted" out on dates? If all he does is text you, tell him he's going to need to find the next you. Send him this reply: "While you're lazily sending me text messages, someone is busy taking me out on dates. That touch screen is all you'll ever touch." Even with email, social networking and text messaging, a gentlewoman still prefers properly being asked on a nice date. Cut communication until you're courted. Insist on real dates. You're in control of this thing. Take your crown back!

Text Tips:

Be Clear – It's easy to misinterpret text. You can't gage emotion, tone or pitch through a phone screen. Be straightforward. Be understandable.

No Substituting Text for Real Communication – Texting is informal. Don't send funeral arrangements, wedding invites, breakup, etc. via text. Such information should be addressed in person or over the phone. Have some decency.

Don't Send Sensitive Information – Social security numbers, bank information and any data you wouldn't want in the hands of a stranger shouldn't be sent…this includes your nude photos. If your phone gets lost or stolen, a stranger now has access to your privates. It's best to deliver sensitive information over a call or in person. With the increase in technological advances, never has it been easier for hackers to gain entry into your phone. Be wise. Be warned.

Reply Back – It's rude to not respond. It can be taken the wrong way. A simple "I'm busy" is sufficient. A one-word response doesn't mean a person is uninterested – it means she/he is busy. Be more concerned with no response.

NOTE: Sending two unanswered text messages is persistence. Sending three unanswered text messages is desperation. Sending four unanswered text messages is stalking. Settle down.

Disclaimer: Your lips can begin a relationship–your breath can end one. If you have bad breath, you should only be allowed to text.

Online Etiquette: Some people believe the Internet is a make-believe magical place for them to become whomever they want and say whatever they want. Just like real life, the Internet requires etiquette.

- o Speak to people online exactly how you'd speak to them in their face. In today's climate, keyboard courage can get you killed.
- o Your online life should reflect your real life. Your status update shouldn't say, "Hang gliding over Italy," when I just saw you at Burger King ordering a #3 with no onions.
- o If you're handling business online, pay no attention to a troll.

Restroom Etiquette: To many women, a restroom isn't merely a setting to deplete waste. It's an environment to fellowship, cry and buy time to dial your friend to instruct her to call you back in five minutes in order to save you from a bad date. The problem isn't what occurs in the restroom–it's what doesn't occur. Post-restroom hand washing is a dying trend. That hand delivered fecal matter is a no-no. It's not only classless, but it's responsible for the spread of harmful bacteria. Get back to the basics, people.
As a younger man, I had my share of run-ins in the Ladies' restroom. Whether it was sneaking in to make out with a young Lady or the combination of a vacant lavatory and my uncontrollable bladder, I've visited enough women's washrooms to witness what a man should never witness. Please learn the protocol of properly discarding personal sanitary items. A code of excellent etiquette is leaving environments that you occupy better off than when you arrived. Clean up after yourself.

Flatulence Etiquette: Part of living is farting and Ladies do it as much as men–they're just usually not as loud and proud about it. I've never heard my wife fart. Ever. I've never heard my mother fart. Ever. A Lady is a flower. Flowers don't stink. I understand we're all human and our bodies must function. I just can't get past the public passing of gas and many agree. It's OK to be too cute to poot. But if you must release scents from the anus, please excuse yourself from all places where you're not the only one breathing. If there exists no immediate exit, provide a warning before the vile chemicals escape and are inhaled, furthermore identified by the nose of an innocent bystander. If you've got to go, you've got to go. Below are four ways you can pass gas with class:

- **Create a Distraction:** In a car, turn up the radio and roll down the window. If in public, cough, sneeze or talk loudly—anything to detract the attention away from the sound. You can't mask that scent though.

- **Go to a Quiet Place:** There must be some secret soundproof place you can go emit. My wife found it! The restroom, perhaps?

- **Exercise Discretion:** When the stomach bubbles, you're in trouble. You can't run once it's done. It takes seconds for the molecules to disperse and the odor to be detected within close proximity. Utilize your growling stomach as a cue to depart expeditiously.

- **Use Your Poker Face:** Don't react. If a tree falls in a forest and no one is around to hear it, does it make a sound? OK, maybe the philosophical thought doesn't work here. What will work is no reaction from you. Only a brave woman has the audacity to fart with a straight face as if it never happened. If you're bold enough to do that, the victim might begin to question if it actually ever occurred. Consequently you'll be ruled out as a perpetrator.

In all seriousness, embrace what makes you human. There are far greater issues than strange noises followed by thirty seconds of a foul odor. Everybody's doing it!

NOTE: If you consume food slower, you'll take in less air and might pass gas less often.

Gold-Digging Etiquette: There's simply no such thing. Gold-digging isn't a new phenomenon, but it's a pathetic one. To engage in any relationship with the ill intention of deception or establishing material possessions as primary interest is immoral, selfish and classless. Prioritizing financial security over all other factors is a recipe for disaster. A man isn't a financial plan. There's nothing wrong with desiring a fellow with financial security as long as you can create the same without him. The only thing a man you're dating is required to pay you is attention. Wake up from the daydream of a man supplying all your needs while you sit oceanside doing nothing with your life. You have all the potential in you to create that lifestyle for yourself. Your life of security, financial freedom and luxury has nothing to do with a man. If you're considering gold-digging, fill out a job application instead. Get a job…a real one.

NOTE: Men can be gold-diggers, too. Be warned.

Goal-Digging Etiquette: I have a dream that one day all gold-diggers will become goal-diggers. If money is your concern, goal-dig. It's much more respected when it's earned. If you insist on being a groupie, stalk your dreams and let success be your sex!

Gift-Giving Etiquette: Giving is a selfless and natural gesture that satisfies an innate desire. Like many forms of etiquette, it fulfills both the receiver and the giver. Receiving gifts is easy.

Giving gifts – not so much. What do you give, when do you give it and to whom shall you give it to?

What to give: Pay attention. People are pretty blatant about their desires whether spoken or unspoken. Take notice to what they don't have, but obviously need. Some women have a keen sense of awareness in regards to figuring out what's lacking and providing accordingly. Scan their home and notice what's missing. Listen to what interests them. Getting gift ideas from someone's social networking pages is a great idea, too. People post what they like. If you're not up to a scavenger hunt, just ask. Some people don't mind at all. If you prefer to surprise someone with a gift, then ask yourself the following questions:

1.   Is the gift for a man or woman?
2.   What is her/his relationship to you?
3.   What's her/his age?
4.   What's the occasion?
5.   Name three things she/he is currently into – what's their personality?

The answer to the above questions should provide you with the perfect gift idea. Below are a few gifts you might consider giving him:

1.   **Give him a chance**. Maybe you've been unnecessarily reluctant or hard on him. If he's a great catch, return that unanswered text and tell him to call you.
2.   **Give him up**. Letting go just might be the best gift for him and for you. This is an affordable gift and might even save you money!

3. **Give him time**. Maybe he's not where you'd like him to be, but well on his way. He's ambitious, trying and showing progress. Understand when something good is worth the wait. This could be a great gift for both of you. Just keep the receipt.

4. **Do you hate those dirty sneakers he wears**? Would you like him to dress his age? Take him to a tailor and upgrade him! This is your opportunity to "change" us without an argument. Great gift!

5. **The perfect scent makes perfect sense**. Another gift for him that you will benefit from is cologne – *see Tom Ford*.

6. **Wrap your credit card in a box with the note**: "Yours for the day" attached. That would be the day!

7. **Forget Skype and get a flight**. Cash in your frequent flyer miles and gift the two of you a vacation. It costs you nothing and benefits the both of you.

8. **You in a bow**. Just a bow. (Married only).

9. **Get him *BEREOLAESQUE: The Contemporary Gentleman & Etiquette book for the Urban Sophisticate*.** He'll be a better man because of it.

10. **Get her a copy of the book you're currently reading**. Nothing says "I care about you" more than sharing wisdom.

Keep in mind that the best gifts are thoughtful gifts. Sometimes it's not about the money you spend, but the time you spend and thought you spend creating something memorable. And don't underestimate the delivery. Deliver creatively. *A scavenger hunt; concert tickets inside of the artist's CD case; plane tickets inside the glove compartment of a new car.* Well, that might be a bit overboard…unless you preside over a board of directors. In that case, spend freely!

When to give: Birthday | Wedding | Engagement Party | Baby Shower | Housewarming | Graduation | Retirement | Christmas | Special Anniversary | Dinner Party | International Business Trip

Gift-giving isn't limited to special occasions. Give back and volunteer when you can. Give with passion. Give with love. Give without expectation.
NOTE: Just because someone gives you a gift, doesn't require you to give one back. A meaningful "Thank you" will do.

Who to give to: You're not Mrs. Claus. Gift-giving shouldn't require too much thought. Give to whom you can when you can. Family, friends and your significant other fall on this list. But a gift is exactly that a gift. It shouldn't be expected, but it should always be appreciated. And don't feel compelled to give a gift beyond your budget. It doesn't matter if the receiver is wealthy and *has it all*. People enjoy being considered, and the fact that you thought to give something is what counts most.

When you give a gift, give a gift completely. Nice shoes are accompanied with quality cedar shoe trees. Davidoff Cigars with the humidor included. It's no different than a gentleman getting you flowers with the vase. A gift is thoughtful. Make sure it's a complete thought.

Hoarding Etiquette: Emotional attachments to inanimate objects can be dangerous. It's OK to keep a cute collection of coins or stamps or whatever you're into, but to fill your dwelling full of stuff is a reflection of you. Cluttered homes reflect a cluttered mind. Hoarding won't cover the issues you're attempting to run from. Facing issues is the only way to get through issues. If you

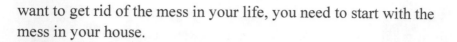

want to get rid of the mess in your life, you need to start with the mess in your house.

Perhaps you're someone who doesn't have a real hoarding issue. But those plastic grocery bags full of other plastic grocery bags that you use as garbage bags…you don't need them. A clean space will grant you peace.

Sex Etiquette: Does there even exist such a thing? Historically, we shy away from the subject because sex is so taboo. We act like sex doesn't happen. Like we all just appeared or were delivered by storks. We position sex in a way that's provocative or procreative, educational or unromantic. Why are we so afraid to talk about something most of the world is doing? Let's have an honest and open discussion about it. It's not bad etiquette to discuss sex. But it's bad sex when you must discuss etiquette.

Etiquette has no place in the bedroom. If you're married, bounce off of the walls, hang from the ceiling fan and leave a few marks. A Lady loves a gentleman who knows when not to be gentle. Pull her chair then pull her hair. Chivalry is foreplay. The same goes for you! Of course it's appropriate to discuss likes and dislikes; what works for you and what doesn't, but formal pleasantries in the bedroom don't make the experience all that pleasant.

My personal view on sex before marriage is that it feels good. My spiritual view on sex before marriage is that it still feels good. The reality is everything that feels good isn't good for you. Sex can be healing, but marriage is the prescription. If you're doing it unwedded, then you're taking an illegal drug. If you're married, feel free to overdose and refuse rehab. Premarital sex won't solve your problems; it'll likely create them. If you're being honest with yourself, premarital sex is putting your body, mind and soul through something it isn't yet prepared for. Sex is a deep spiritual connection intended for the person you're spending the rest of your life with. Soul ties are real. Popular culture and media often portray sex as a casual act to commit with whomever, wherever and whenever it feels right. It often suggests it's OK to follow all of our sexual desires, but fails to inform us of the not-so-obvious consequences. You can end up imprisoned by the very act you thought was a liberating exercise of your freedom. And once you start, it's difficult to stop. Casual sex is like casual cocaine–it won't stay casual. You may be able to escape an STD or pregnancy, but you can't dodge an unwanted soul tie. Sexual connections with someone, or people who are not assigned to your life is what causes you to stay when you know you should leave. It's what allows you to settle when you know you've been done wrong. Dust settles – people don't. When you lay down with something dirty, you get up with something dirty. When you lay down with a man, you can take on his energy. But none of this is considered when alcohol is already flowing through the bloodstream and you've accepted his text to come over at 4 a.m. You ignore all reservations and make reservations at his place. Self-control is more reliable than birth control. Listen to your moral compass even when the alternative feels good. That's what character is. That's what a gentlewoman does. The choice is yours.

THE PRICE FOR SEX IS MARRIAGE...THE PRICE FOR A RELATIONSHIP IS COMMITMENT – IT'S HARD TO ASK A MAN TO PAY FOR EITHER WHEN YOU'RE GIVING BOTH FOR FREE.

I don't publicly condone premarital sex, but if you're getting into it, listen up:

Sex has lost its value with many: People often have sex with people they don't find attractive, cute, kind of cute, average, decent or even tolerable. So stop voluntarily committing yourself to someone who isn't committed to you. Don't barter your goods for someone average. And don't pretend to be a single man's wife. Giving marriage privileges to a boyfriend is like giving an intern the CEO's salary. I wish you the best.

Sex partner ≠ Your Partner: You can make love daily atop Italian Carrara marble countertops to the shadows of a kitchen floor, but if the commitment conversation hasn't come up, you're just a really, really cool friend. Quit committing without a commitment conversation. Common sense says commitment requires consent. If you haven't discussed a relationship, you're in one with yourself. The frequent sex and those dinner dates don't make that man your man. Make sure the two of you are on the same page because he might be referencing an entirely different book.

Sometimes sex just hides everything that's bad about a relationship: Sex is powerful! Good sex can fool you into thinking you're in love with someone you don't even like. If all you have in common is sex, then you really don't have much in common.

Condom courtesy states: if you insist on having sex, insist on having sex safely. Condoms are cheaper than child support and abstinence is free!
NOTE: Every man you lay with has the potential to make you a mother. Sometimes peace of mind trumps piece of man.

Miss Representation

Miss Representation: *The Birth of a Nation*

Element: Woman
Symbol: Wo
Discoverer: Adam
Atomic Weight: Accepted as 115, but known to vary from 100 to 200 lbs.
Occurrence: Surplus quantities in all countries and urban areas alike

Physical Properties
-Boils at nothing, freezes without reason
-Melts if given proper treatment
-Bitter if utilized improperly

Chemical Properties
-Reacts to precious stones
-May explode spontaneously
-Activity greatly increased when absorbed in alcohol

Uses
-Most powerful money-reducing agent known
-Great aid to pleasure

Test
-Turns green if placed adjacent to exceptional specimen

Caution
-Fragile
-Handle at your own risk

THIS IS SADLY HOW MILLIONS OF WOMEN ARE VIEWED

Miss,

You are a representation of a misrepresentation with limitless expectations. You're expected to be a pure virgin, yet birth babies and look cute while doing it. You should be a stay-at-home mom while working a six-figure job, be independent yet depend on men, and dress like a Lady of the night, but dare not be one. What type of message is this? Google the word "beauty" without the safe search option and notice the images that arise–thousands of thin pale women, some even nude, in compromising positions. Open your favorite magazine, turn to your dearest television show and you'll notice the same trend. They try to devalue you. It's a full-time business. Once they have access to your mind, they have access to your money. Don't accept that rhetoric. Don't believe that hype.

It's not man or magazine's job to make you feel worthy. Our culture raises women to be confused and insecure. A man will tell you 31 things he dislikes about you, leave you and go date another woman with the same 31 flaws, plus one. It's not man or makeup's job to make you feel beautiful. To seek validation is to give people and things permission to determine your value. You must acknowledge and walk in your own splendor. Confidence isn't based upon compliments. It comes from an understanding of your worth and significance–none of which comes from people or *People Magazine*. Arrogance comes from the crazy love you have for yourself–confidence comes from the crazy love God has for you. History is made in the womb. Your Creator determined you were beautiful enough to be born. You're worthy; you're significant; you're beautiful. You came into the world that way. Anything else is a lie.

"There are 3 billion women who don't look like supermodels & only 8 who do." – **The Body Shop**

A lie is as effective as the truth if you believe it and act on it. If cute with a side of skinny were an option on the menu at creation's drive-thru, heaven would sell out. Everyone's fitting in and no one's standing out. There's a strange obsession to be normal in our communities. What is normal? Does normal involve looking and sounding like everyone else? Being a child of God makes normal impossible. Acceptance is the most highly sought after commodity. However, you weren't born for people's approval. You were formed with purpose, on purpose. You don't have a mole by happenstance or a wide nose unintentionally. Your ailment isn't an accident. I told you, you were born beautiful. There are no ugly women – only careless women. You weren't created to feel inadequate or to be arrogant. People will judge you based on their own insecurities and limitations. You're never as bad as they say you are and you're never as perfect as they say you are. So don't look up to see who's cheering or booing, just keep going. Your life is your own and it's specifically designed to be lived by you.

Women who fit in hardly stand out. Celebrate authenticity and unapologetically be you.

Lose the lies. Disregard the comments section. People must earn the right to criticize you. No matter your bad habits, mistakes or disappointments, it's never too late to accept your reality–you're God's masterpiece. You're beloved. You're chosen. You're an overcomer. No one can do what you've been called to do better than you because your only competition is in the mirror. Life begins when you believe you are who God says you are.

A WOMAN IS HER BEST WHEN SHE'S JUST BEING A WOMAN.

But it's not enough to know your worth. Live your worth! You must behave like you know what you're worth. Not everyone will comprehend that worthiness is a birthright. Prove them wrong, but do so in an admirable manner. Arrogance isn't a reflection of knowing your worth. Being bourgeois isn't a display of significance. It's the opposite, actually. To display worthiness means to conduct oneself with honorable intent—with manners and class. Act like you know who you are and whose you are.

It doesn't matter your story; breathing is a sign of worthiness.

The whore is as worthy as the queen. Don't allow society's judgment to confuse you. God's truth is often the world's fiction. Acting on your sexual desires doesn't decrease your worth. You can't *ride* your way from God's love. The One who designed you determined your value. Greater than nature's beauty, sunsets, oceans and waterfalls, you are God's masterpiece. You're far more beautiful than the Mona Lisa or Mozart's music. Now act like it. Don't let little lies grant access to your lovely life. Your worth can't be diminished by your life choices. God's love isn't conditional. You're always worthy. It's up to you to accept this. It's impossible to believe in God without believing what He says about you.

You were formed with the Creator's definition of beauty. Somewhere along the line, society changed that definition. But you weren't created for anyone to define. God looks at you and sees purpose–not what others tell you that you are. To worry about what everyone thinks about you is the quickest way to forget who you are. People-pleasing is idolatry.

As men, we might attempt to degrade you. An elder has to ask us, "What if that was your mother?" or "You wouldn't treat your sister that way." It's a shame you have to be viewed as family to be valued. You've been lied to. The moment God created you is the moment you became worthy.

You're a Lady with design and purpose, not just some girl with a designer purse. Class can't be purchased. People should be able to tell what you stand for by the way you carry yourself, not the purse you carry. Self-love, self-esteem, self-respect and "self"-confidence – all of these words become more powerful when "self" comes first. That's not selfish. You must love yourself in order to love others and respect yourself in order to respect others.

Insecurity is known to penetrate through any level of confidence. The voice that ruins most dreams is your own. Wounds heal, but unresolved issues don't - Don't be scared to get scarred. Stare at your scars until they become beautiful. They're reminders. You're only a victim if you don't get back up. Don't let anyone or anything take your power.

*"I'm Beautiful." -**You***

God created man, but He constructed woman.

PRETTY GIRLS

It's tragic that being pretty has become one of society's coveted honors. It's like winning a Nobel Peace Prize. Some women gather together, pop champagne corks and toast to being cute as if it's cause for celebration. This type of behavior should be illegal. A judge needs to throw the book at them–the *Gentlewoman* book.

Oh, and your cute friends don't automatically make you cute. Osmosis only works in science. Pour out that champagne and keep reading.

Pretty might open doors, but intellect lets you in – Don't be stuck outside with your pretty ass.

Pretty is what you are, but beauty is what you do with it. Have you ever been to a highly promoted party that ended up being completely empty inside? Well, that's what it's like when you're sexy, but dumb. It's similar to the anticipation built up from an amazing movie trailer, only for the movie to be a complete disappointment. A pretty face is cool, but the mind is God's masterpiece. You become boring when you're unaccompanied by intellect. At this point, being smart is actually cuter than being cute. What you look like will never be as important as what you do. Be so good that you can't be ignored. You're here for an instant. What will you do with that time?

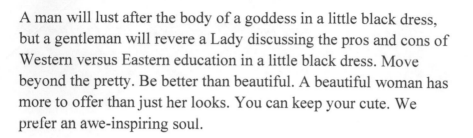

A man will lust after the body of a goddess in a little black dress, but a gentleman will revere a Lady discussing the pros and cons of Western versus Eastern education in a little black dress. Move beyond the pretty. Be better than beautiful. A beautiful woman has more to offer than just her looks. You can keep your cute. We prefer an awe-inspiring soul.

AN UGLY MIND ATTRACTS AN UGLY PERSON...ENJOY YOUR DATE!

There exists too many gorgeous, down-to-earth women for you to ever be cute with an attitude. Being attractive doesn't provide a pass to be rude. Pretty isn't enough. Humble yourself. Does it ever cross your mind that maybe your looks aren't for your personal vanity, but to draw others in for your life's purpose? Maybe it's not all about you after all. Perhaps you were granted good looks for a purpose greater than you and your arrogance. If you don't know the purpose of something, you'll misuse it. When God builds, He builds with purpose. Please don't misuse your pretty. Gain comfort in it. Accept it. Figure it out. But don't misuse it. If a genuine smirk will get you out of a speeding ticket or earn you a discounted meal, by all means go ahead and smile with those pretty eyes. Solely relying on the use of sexuality as currency is prostitution. Check the definition for yourself. Just don't be selfishly beautiful.

Get beyond the plastic look. You're not a doll. If you were to get a knife and cut a doll's head off, you would find no brain inside. If you were to make a small incision on the doll's chest, there would be no soul. A human lacking these two vital components is in a severe vegetative state. You're a living, breathing manifestation of the most compelling dimension of life. Good looks without intellect is a Bentley with no gas, a wallet with no cash and a stripper with no—well, you get the point. Over time, your mind and spirit stand out more than your long hair and lipstick…congratulations if you have all four. But if you mimic the persona of a lifeless doll, we'll naturally assume you want to be played. "All you are is pretty" has got to be the worst compliment ever. We'd rather have a Lady with Bachelor of Science stamped on her degree than *Mattel* stamped on her tail. What's your worth?

For what it's worth, you couldn't pay for it. No job, degree or salary will cover the cost. You might receive rewards, status and luxury for those carnal accomplishments, but that's not the real measure of your worth. Your true worth is the value of your soul.

Ephesians 2:10 says she's God's masterpiece… but she still searches for likes on online.

Do You Care What Men Think?

Benecia Williams
Fashion Stylist

I believe everyone cares about what someone thinks. There's motivation behind what we do as a whole. Although it may not be the immediate driving force, there's always an influence. Let me be very clear, I am a woman. It will never matter how calloused or disconnected from emotion I've mastered to be [at any given time]; I care about my perception from the man's perspective. This perspective does not dictate my womanly responsibility, but it sheds light on my overall behavior and this is a reflection of how I carry myself. For me, it's better to be safe than sorry. I'm a very traditional, paint-inside-the-lines kind of woman. I believe in the theories of being a Lady: Cross the legs at the ankles, stand with your legs together, never cut a man at the knees kind of theory. It's not for everyone, but I'd like to remain a woman, not a woMAN. Because perception is no longer independently exclusive, practicing a more respectable behavior isn't a negative. Who really wants to be discussed in the same conversation as harlot just because I own the freedom of expression and I can abuse it if I want to, yet still remain who I believe I am in MY head? My mother used to always tell me, "If you want people to know who you are, you show them." You must be a walking, talking testimony to who you want to be at all times. That's sheer discipline and control. That's a gentlewoman!

Ben Wills is a men's wardrobe consultant; she's worked with celebrities, athletes and artists. Ben is the editor of TheWellDressedMan.net and creator of the Well Dressed Initiative used to present mentorship between males and encourage young men in putting their best foot forward.

Inner Views

Inner Views: *Interviews*

Meagan Good
Award-Winning Actress | Producer

Define femininity?

1. *Femininity is self-love. Loving all of your perfect imperfections. Understanding your immeasurable beauty inside and out. Loving the skin and the being that God created you to be as a woman.*

You represent a woman of faith who expresses herself in a very contemporary way. Some might call it sexual. What do you say about that?

2. *I'm most definitely a woman of Faith. I love Jesus Christ with all of my heart and with every essence of my being. As a Christian and within "our" society, we're taught certain levels of appropriateness [like dressing up for church]. But I prefer arriving comfortably. I don't believe that God requires us to dress up for Him. I like being able to lift my hands and praise without the restriction of a tight jacket. I like being able to get on my knees if I want to [without the restriction of a skirt or dress]. I believe that He loves us no matter what we wear and no matter how we come. As we seek Him, if He has an issue with the way that we're carrying (or dressing) ourselves, I believe He will reveal it to us if we're willing to hear Him. I'm not one who worries much about what's appropriate by man's standards. Man's*

opinion of appropriateness sways often depending on the circumstance. Although I never intend or wish to offend anybody, I'm more concerned about what my heavenly Father thinks of me. And I believe that the word of God is true when it states that man looks at the appearance, but God looks at the heart. I think if we had God's eyes, we would focus more on people's hearts instead of often turning people off from Christianity altogether by being very judgmental about appearances and other things.

How did you approach dating before you met your husband?

3. *Before I met my husband I always approached dating with my number one rule: whomever I dated had to believe in Christ. I didn't want to waste any time going down a road where we would be unequally yoked. Though I was very specific on that point, I lacked in other areas. I tried often to be celibate, but hadn't given the commitment to abstinence the real effort it deserved. I always made excuses and felt that God knew my heart. After doing that for so long, you begin to understand if you expect a different result and you're doing the same things, it's the definition of insanity. So I decided to do something different, and as a result, I got a completely different result...the best one I could've ever imagined in my life :)*

You were a woman who seemed to have all that she wanted except a husband. What would you say to successful women who struggle with that thought?

4. *I would tell women who appear to be successful in their own right and haven't met their husband yet, to be patient.*

Trust God's timing. His timing is always perfect. If I had hooked up with my husband sooner in my life, I would've messed it up. I wasn't ready. I needed everything that happened in between to prepare me for marriage and prepare me for this time of my life. I have no reservations and no regrets. Although there were some things I would've done differently, everything taught me something and made me better, not bitter. I'm thankful and completely attentive to this season in my life–especially my marriage because His timing was perfect.

How has etiquette been instrumental in your relationship?

5. *Having etiquette is instrumental because it shows a level of class that is to be respected. We're all a work in progress, but how we carry ourselves demonstrates "how" we are to be treated. In some circumstances we're still full of potential, even in the midst of our mess. It proposes first-hand insight to what we will and will not allow. In the beginning stages, etiquette can even paint the picture of what kind of woman we generally are.*

Does the past define you?

6. *The past absolutely does not define me. It's only assisted in leading me in the way I believe I was created to go.*

If you had a daughter and could leave her a final message on your deathbed, what would you say?

7. *I would tell her above everything to love herself because she is God's perfect creation. And to pray for "His" eyes to*

see herself the way that He sees her so that her sight will guide her self-worth, decisions and actions.

If you could write a letter to your younger self, what would it say?

8. *Dear Meagan,*
   Your heavenly father is proud of you, so don't make decisions assuming that you've already disappointed him. Remember, there will be more people in your life that last only for a season and the ones who are for a lifetime. Don't make decisions for seasonal approval. Even people who love you may not want you to succeed. When people's time has expired in your life – let them go. Don't let people abuse your kindness. If they can't love you beyond you standing up for yourself, then they weren't meant to. God's plan is better than your dreams and often connected. Don't take everything personal. Sometimes people's problem with you is really their problem with themselves. Give grace because you'll need it, too. And know that your husband will see you with eyes as close to God's as you can get on this earth. Don't settle for falling in love because you will fall a few times in your lifetime. Instead, arrive at what God has divinely chosen for you.

   Meagan Good is an American film and television actress and occasional film producer.

Bryan-Michael Cox

Grammy Award-Winning Super Producer | Platinum Songwriter | GA Music Hall of Fame Inductee

You believe in chivalry. You've written songs like "Let's Get Married" by Jagged Edge and "Just Be a Man About it" by Toni Braxton. Is etiquette a deal breaker in your relationships?

1. *Etiquette is absolutely a deal breaker in my relationships. A woman should be a woman. I want her to be kept and to keep herself up. Your relationship represents you. If I'm taking you to Nobu restaurant and people know who I am and take pictures of you and me together, you've got to represent. I'm not saying she shouldn't have her own stuff. We need women. Women are brilliant. Women motivate us to get to that next level. When a man finds a woman, he finds a good thing—the right woman, obviously. Etiquette is very important. Being from the south, I'm going to always show etiquette. I'm a 'yes ma'am,' open the door and pay the bill kind of guy. So I expect whoever I'm spending time with to have the same kind of etiquette. That womanly etiquette.*

What's your biggest turn-off with a woman?

2. *Lack of depth. Lack of intelligent depth. If we can't maintain a conversation for more than five to ten minutes, there's no depth. There's nothing we can talk about. I like to talk and there are a billion things going on in this world—we should have something to discuss. If we don't*

100

have anything to talk about, then what are we doing sitting here and having dinner spending my money?

What is the greatest misconception that women have about men?

3. *The greatest misconception that women have about men is that they can change us. Internally, how a person is how a person is. They can evolve. They can add things to their repertoire to make them better. I always say this: Money magnifies who you are. If you're an arrogant and selfish a-hole, when you get money you'll just be a bigger version of that. If you're a generous and kind person, when you get money you'll be a larger and better version of that. Who you are to the core is who you are and I don't think there's any changing that.*

The other greatest misconception is that they think we want them to change. I like the Lady I met. If she was wild & crazy when we got together, that shouldn't change. I don't give a damn how many kids we have. That shouldn't change. We should adapt to our time and figure it out. If we have kids now, we can't be hanging off the ceiling in the living room anymore. And men can't change women either. In our initial conversations, women tell us who they are. If a woman says, "Oh, I'm not really domestic; I despise all things domestic; cooking isn't really my thing," she's not gonna cook, doc. She told you early. If that's what you're looking for in a woman, she's told you she's not going to do that. Pay attention to the details. A lot of times we give people the benefit of the doubt when they tell you straight

*up whom they are and what they're going to do. I've
learned, there's no benefit in doubt.*

What do you teach your son about women?

4. *I teach my son that he should always be honest. I think
where men go wrong with women is not being honest. If
you know you're not ready to be in a monogamous
relationship, you have to be honest about that. Cheating is
such a big issue because of expectations–unrealistic
expectations that aren't even talked about. If you're honest,
you never know what kind of concessions a woman will
give for honesty. Even if it's just for a moment and they
decide they'd rather not deal with you anymore. At least
you gave them the option–they have the choice. A lot of
times men don't give women that choice. We say, "I love
you; I want to be with you; you're the only one and I'm
never going to cheat on you." We might not even say that;
we just give the illusion. When you say that, they believe
you. Then they say, "Oh, I'm going to marry him because
I'm in love with him and he's in love with me." But in
reality, you have another phone and you've got another
life. And that's the hurt! That's where the hurt is–that's
where the hurt resides because you never gave her a
choice. She didn't have the chance to say that's not what
she wants to do or she's not going to do that. But you
wanted to have your cake and eat it, too. You were selfish.
You baited her in, she gave you her all and that's how you
repay her? When really, if you were honest from the gate
and said, "Listen, this is the kind of man I am...I'm a
gentleman and I'll treat you right, but I've got this, this and
this," you give women the opportunity to make the choice.*

*Even if they decide not to be with you, you've got their
respect. You could have led them down a path that they
weren't ready to get led down, but you were honest and she
was able to make a decision not to deal with that. And you
don't know what will be birthed from that respect. You both
might end up getting what you want anyway.*

Bryan-Michael Cox is Billboard Magazine's #1 Music Producer. His credits
include Usher, Mariah Carey, Sean "Diddy" Combs, Whitney Houston, The
Isley Brothers, Destiny's Child, Janet Jackson, Jessica Simpson, Jennifer Lopez,
Fergie, Alicia Keys, Aaliyah, Justin Bieber, Chris Brown & many more. Cox
eclipsed the record previously held by the Beatles for Billboard's most
consecutive #1 hits.

Leola "Tinker" Bell
Playboy Playmate | Miss February 2012

How much value do you place on your exterior appearance?

1. *I've based my entire career on my external appearance.
   Even as a child, I'd try to emulate my mother from how she
   walked, to the perfume she'd wear and the products she'd
   use in her hair. It's so crazy, but I even used my Barbie
   dolls as a guide. I come from a southern family, where
   more emphasis is placed on beauty and grace, and
   everything else falls a close second. I'm definitely not
   saying that's a good thing, but as a child it shaped my
   views on how a woman was supposed to look, speak and
   act.*

What has embracing sexuality done for you?

2. *Made me a Lone Ranger! I don't think many people, including both men and women, know what it means to truly embrace their sexuality. I see my friends at the clubs (at our chosen celebrity host's table for the night) and their idea of embracing their sexuality is, "Let's go home with them." Instant tire screech for me. It's not about being promiscuous. I'm not going to lie; it's a play land in Miami. We have access to people, places and experiences most don't. But embracing my sexuality is acknowledging that I am a woman. A real woman who can take care of my household while holding onto a gift so special, that I truly feel it radiates from inside me. So I don't have to drop it low to show people I embrace who I am. I've always been fascinated by sex, by f***king, by making love...But that's not embracing my sexuality. Embracing my sexuality is being comfortable in my own skin. Being able to talk about my love for all things sensual and erotic. Everything has its time and place, and it's made me such a free spirit. It effects more than your sex life. You don't even have to have an active sex life to embrace that.*

How did you overcome the stereotypes and judgment thrown your way?

3. *That's actually something I struggled hard with at first. I have the blessing and the curse of being extremely sensitive. However, I knew when I made the choice to start modeling that I would be judged more than others. When I made the decision to pose for Playboy I knew what people would say. I just had no idea to the extent they would take*

104

it. I had Christian groups devote full website threads to talk about my fall from grace and how disgusting it was to display my body in such a way. I had women attacking me from every angle. I had a past acquaintance release a very private video of me without my consent. It me hurt badly and hurt my family, which hurt even more. It caused me to question every life decision I had made. Then one day, I had an epiphany. WHO CARES! I posed nude for the number one, best-selling gentleman's magazine in the world. In a beautiful and artistic way. To be the 700th playmate and the 25th black playmate meant something to me. To be in a sorority with Marilyn Monroe the first playmate meant something to me. She was chastised and revered in her own time. Why would I let people's uneducated opinions rule my life? I'm a grown woman and I do whatever I want. This made me stronger. My tears and anger helped build my shield that I now carry with me on a daily. But I carry it with a smile. True freedom comes in being carefree enough not to care, but wise enough to make the decisions best for me. I'm much happier for it.

How are you able to balance sexuality with class?

4. *Having a strong, beautiful and southern mother as a role model taught me to carry myself with class as a daily thing. It's in my actions, it's how I walk, talk; and speak. My sexuality is who I am. Can't escape it; I embrace it. I choose to reveal it.*

If you had a daughter, how would you feel if she posed for Playboy?

5. *I don't think it was my parent's dream for me to become a playmate centerfold. My father being a pastor and my mother a true southern belle. But fortunately for me, my parents love me, their daughter. They don't have to love my actions. I chose the path less traveled, but both paths lead to the same destination. If my daughter chose my same occupation, I would be proud of her strength. I would be proud she loved herself and her body enough to show the world, "Here I am and I'm free!" I would be very happy. Like mother like daughter they always say...*

If you were to write a letter to your younger self, what would you say?

6. *I have some news for you. Your life won't be easy, but it'll be worth it. I wish I could tell you to stay away from this or from that, from him or her. But why? In life we all have to endure our own journey. Sometimes you'll feel God has abandoned you, but He'll always be there. Cling to Him, baby girl. Even when you feel you're not worthy of His grace, it's there for you!! Please don't let what others who don't matter in your life dictate your actions. Set goals for yourself and never become complacent. You are meant for great things! Take the time to get to know you. Don't be afraid to go to dinner alone. Please for your sake girl, learn Spanish. You'll need it. You end up in Miami. Embrace your natural hair. Men don't like weaves as much as you do! Ha! Don't be afraid to let your husband know sex is essential and that you'll crave it more than most. It's*

how your brain will get things done. Trust me! Haha! Love yourself first before you try to love anyone else. Your order is God, husband and if you have any, then children. Oh yeah, stay away from working at that restaurant you'll interview for. You'll gain 50 pounds and it's a mission working that off. Haha! I love you.

Leola Bell is a Playboy Playmate, Miss February 2012 and a preacher's daughter. She has a degree psychology.

Bobby Wagner
NFL Linebacker | ESPY Award nominee | Sports Illustrated Defensive Rookie of the Year

Is it important for the Lady you date to have etiquette? Why/Why not?

1. *It matters if you're really interested in her. When you're just trying to have sex, you really don't care. As long as she's not crazy, you really don't care how she conducts herself. But if it's a woman you consider having a family with, I feel like you pay more attention to things like that.*

You're a star NFL Linebacker. You have women at your disposal. In a sea of women, what captures your attention?

2. *A woman who conducts herself differently than every other woman. I'm attracted to a woman that looks like she would present a challenge to get to know her. Being an NFL player, you do get exposed to a lot of women where it really*

doesn't take much to get their number or get them to come over and do whatever. So I think that women that kind of blow you off the first time and then you see them out again, it's a real challenge. But there's a fine line between being a challenge and not really being interested.

What's your biggest turn-off with women of this generation?

3. *Lack of privacy. This day and age, a lot of women are so caught up in social media. That's really not attractive to me. We can be vibing and be all good and then we end up getting in a fight over something whether it's a picture or something along those lines. I think my career influences it just a little bit, but I think it'd still be somewhat like that if I worked at Starbucks. I think it's something everyone deals with. In the old days (I say "old" like I'm old), the minute you start talking to a girl or you're interested and she likes you – she'd go back and tell her friends about how great the date was. But now, you're not just going on a date with just her; you're going on a date with the rest of the world.*

What is the greatest misconception that women have about men?

4. *If you're an attractive male, I feel like most women automatically assume you have a lot of women and you have sex a lot. In most cases, some won't even talk to you because of that assumption. It's kind of the same mindset with a lot of guys. If they see an attractive woman, they won't approach her because they feel like a lot of men already approached her. Or they won't tell her she's beautiful because she's probably heard it. An attractive*

*woman won't approach because she doesn't want to seem like "**that**" girl. She doesn't want to come off like all the other "**thirsty**" girls by telling him he looks good. But if an attractive woman came up to me and said I was attractive, I would say, "Finally there's a woman who's not afraid to come up and speak." I don't have a problem with women approaching me. I think it's actually cool because a lot of women expect the guys to do that, so they just don't do it. I like a woman who's bold and also like a woman who subtlety drops hints.*

If you could speak on a loudspeaker in front of millions of women for ten seconds, what would you say?

5. *Stay classy, the good man will find you. I say that because some women already are classy or might be church girls and they see all the other girls throwing their ass and stuff. Those girls get the guys they want, so some of the classy women feel like that's what they've got to do.*

Bobby Wagner is an American football linebacker for the Seattle Seahawks of the National Football League. He played college football at Utah State. He was considered one of the best linebacker prospects for the 2012 NFL Draft.

Interlude
Love Letters

3 Roses: *Lost Mail*

The most Googled word on the Internet is "love." It seems you're searching in all the wrong places

If you think an extended text message is a love letter, you're a product of modern times. Unfortunately, the likelihood of you experiencing a genuine handwritten note is as low as a lace front wig hairline. The handwritten note is still a courteous gesture in the land of texts and emails. Love Letters are the most beautiful, but abandoned and underrated forms of communication hardly written.

After traveling the country speaking to generations of gentlewomen, I understand how important it is for you to hear this. You need love. Not that get-you-pregnant-kind of love, but that tender love that only a brother, father or friend could give. I sent this out to you years ago, but somehow it got lost in the mail…

This is my Love Letter:

Dear Gentlewomen,

I love you. I mean that from the bottom of my heart. I didn't write this for recognition or a pat on the back. I get that at home. I wrote this for you.

I want you to freely explore and express your beauty however you decide. But with 18-year-olds having Botox parties, breast implants and tummy tucks, it's difficult for me to believe you're comfortable in your own beauty.

Society has skewed your perception. Each channel you flip and page you turn, you're either witnessing an airbrushed woman or a

111

made-up one. Don't compare yourself to an edited image. We don't need you Photoshopped–give us your flaws and we'll touch you up. Not in a filthy way. But in a loving way because those blemishes are beyond compare. Don't be afraid of your natural self. Beauty is because beauty is. Beauty doesn't try; it's externally reflected from the internal. Beauty is uncontrollable and in its most natural state, beauty is you.

The mirror isn't merely for vanity. Self-reflection can free you from yourself. Take a deep look in the mirror–it's the most honest companion you might ever have. Sooner or later you'll have to come to terms with yourself. It's painful to deal with pain, but your outer view needs an interview with your inner view. Excessively taking care of the exterior in attempt to cover the pain on the interior is like painting over a filthy car. You've got to wash it clean. You'd like you more if you loved you more. Figure out who you are, fall in love with that person and don't apologize for it. Confidence is simply freedom from doubt.

Matthew 6:25 says, "The important things in life aren't things…" Expensive bags, excessive makeup, nails done, hair done and everything done won't make you beautiful. Somewhere along the way, you lost your attractive innocence. It's tragic if your father gave you your first orgasm, mother may have neglected you or your boyfriend might've beaten you. Abandonment and abuse may have made you believe the lie that you're not whole; that you're not amazing just the way you are. You can't fill your voids with things or second-rate sex. Only love can fill your holes, but you must accept love. Trust your struggle. It'll be used in a mighty way to touch lives in manners you can't imagine. That's beautiful. You're so beautiful–no matter what they say and no matter what

you've been through. You're glowing. You don't need permission
to be yourself.

Gentlemen, this is for you: I know some of you snuck off and
read this and I don't blame you, so listen up. Just because you go
together doesn't mean she knows you still think she's beautiful.
It's not your job to create confidence, but your attention to, and
awareness of her is essential. Reassurance is your relationship
insurance–pay weekly. A woman has to battle daily thoughts of not
being enough, no longer satisfying us, not being attractive enough
and other women taking our attention. Secure her, no makeup, the
pure her. Your woman is beautiful art – go to her art show and
gaze; leave your praise in the comment box to remind her how
perfect she is just the way she is

And ladies, please understand you don't *need* a man to tell you
you're amazing. All you need is a mirror.

Yours truly,

Enitan Bereola, II

Dear Cinderella, Snow White and Sleeping Beauty,

I am writing this letter to you as a man you may be unfamiliar with
– a father. It seems the only men you have encountered are princes

villains who wants to kill you or dwarfs who
her's job is to guide, mold, protect, inform,
...u impart. Since you might have not had an active
rather in your life, I'm going adopt you along with the wonderful
daughters I already have.

When your younger sisters read about your lives, they seemed to
be summed up in twenty pages or less with more pictures than
words. That's a problem because boys often see more than they
listen. It's very important that you don't just paint a picture for a
man, but give room to hear his words. If he can't articulate how he
sees himself and you in the future, turn the page. If he has all
emotion and no intellect, turn the page. If he can't read, SHUT
THE BOOK!

Most of your lives seem to omit courtship and go straight to a big
event like a ball or a party. A lot your sisters following your
example have become messed up as a result. They spend all of
their lives dreaming about a wedding, but never preparing for a
marriage. Don't expend all your energy on finding the perfect dress
when you don't have an address. The color of the flowers doesn't
matter if you haven't been open about finances, and the reception
should be cancelled if you and your future spouse haven't been real
with one another.

All three of you come from broken homes or dysfunctional
families, but you never seem to address in your book how that
could influence your mindset. Take the good pieces from what's
broken and build something good. A broken diamond will make
many wonderful rings. A broken leg will often heal and become
stronger than it initially was, but a broken vow, a broken promise
and a broken heart can cause more harm than good if not properly

dealt with. Make up in your mind that as you move forward you won't repeat dysfunctional patterns, habits and mindsets that you witnessed in childhood. The worst mistake in the world is the one you never learn from.

In your stories there is no evidence that any of you ever worked again after you found love. Love is never unemployed. Love should make you want to work on your dreams, work on your passion and work on yourself. The sum total of love is not a shopping spree and trips–but goals, unity, family and focus. The benefit of love is that you no longer work alone, but you now work alongside someone who wants to see you accomplish everything your heart desires.

Now the bad news: there are no fairy godmothers. The good news is that there is a God! Establish an authentic relationship with Him and you will find how to have one with yourself. A relationship with God will teach you sacrifice, devotion, commitment, faithfulness, discipline, forgiveness, understanding and expectation. When you see how God loves you it will give you a manual on how you should love and be loved. If the person you have interest in doesn't love God, it will be impossible for them to be able to love you.

As I close this letter, I want you to know I ripped out the last pages of your books because they said, "Happily ever after." While I want all of you to be happy forever, I don't want you to be taken by surprise when life happens – bills will come, sickness may arrive, disagreements will take place and children will add stress. But if you love each other, remember there will be more mountains than valleys.

Always remember life isn't a fairy tale; it's a reality show!

Love,

Dad

Dr. Jamal-Harrison Bryant
Father of Four Daughters, Pastor of 8,000

Dear Sisters,

When did we forget we are queens? I see a lot of women being talked to, talked at and handled any kind of way and it just pisses me off. Back in the day we were WOMEN! Our mere presence demanded respect and not a single word was even spoken! It was the way we carried ourselves, the way we dressed, the way we spoke to others and our speech was soft, yet heard – gentle, yet firm. Now women are loud, sassy, dress however and allow men to treat them as objects to be tossed aside at their leisure. There's no value in today's woman and we need to take our value back!

With Love,

Alesha Reneé
BET Host/Actress

Your roses mean something. Each bloom is significant, but together, the three specifically symbolize the words: *I love you.*

Decoding Roses:

Always wonderful and always pretty, roses bring any home or office alive. Did you know that the quantities of roses you receive have significance? Allow me to explain:

> **1 Rose:** Love at first sight on date one. Later in the relationship it says, 'I still love you.' We can spend $50 to $70 on a dozen roses for sheer spectacle, but the ultimate gesture of devotion is a single rose.
>
> **2 Roses:** Mutual feelings. If roses are intertwined, it's even more beautiful.
>
> **3 Roses:** I love you.
>
> **5 Roses:** Just a couple degrees up from the aforementioned, five roses says, 'I love you very much.'
>
> **6 Roses:** Infatuation
>
> **10 Roses:** You're perfect.
>
> **12 Roses:** Will you be mine?
>
> **13 Roses:** Forever friends.
>
> **15 Roses:** I'm sorry. (*You don't want to get these too often*).
>
> **20 Roses:** Sincere feelings; no games.
>
> **21 Roses:** I'm committed; dedicated
>
> **24 Roses:** Always on my mind…twenty-four hours a day.
>
> **36 Roses:** So in love; head over heels.
>
> **40 Roses:** My love is genuine.
>
> **44 Roses:** My love is constant and unchanging.
>
> **50 Roses:** A love that knows no bounds and has never been regretted.
>
> **99 Roses:** I love you until death.
>
> **100 Roses:** Total devotion. Not to say he isn't devoted without the gesture; this is just reinforcement of the notion.

King's English

King's English: *A Lady's Lexicon*

Her lips are pleasing, but the beauty doesn't only exist for aesthetic fulfillment – they rest in place to protect the most powerful tool you possess. Words, words, words. There's something so arousing about words. You play with them allowing them space to dance within your mind. You construct them to your liking until selflessly giving away to your listener for access, interpretation and thought. They drip on pondering ears and take on a life of their own. You can progress a nation or summon an army with a couple quick thrusts of your tongue. Taking full control over words can mean the difference between poor or rich, hopeless or ebullient and death or life.

"Politeness is the art of choosing among one's real thoughts." **-Abel Stevens**

A Lady shouldn't be judged by her inability to produce graceful phrases, but a well-spoken woman deserves handclaps. Her name alone should be draped over the shoulders of the greats or inhaled on the necks of lovers. Her moniker is a high-end fashion line or designer fragrance waiting to happen.

OK, maybe not all that, but fluency of language is gorgeous. It suggests a higher level of intellect and reflects a healthy desire to learn more. However, not taking control of your native language is an embarrassment to it.

GRAMMAR: Simply put, grammar is a set of rules governing what is allowable in a language. Aren't there enough rules? You don't want the grammar police monitoring your every word and correcting each error, but excessive abuse of your language requires correction. Allow me:

- If you use "For all intensive purposes" in an argument, you just lost that argument. Put your guard down and pick your dictionary up.
- We appreciate your appreciation, but "Congrads" isn't a word.
- All losses are tragic—especially followed by the phrase, "Sorry for your lost."
- If someone needs clarification and asks you to be more "Pacific," kindly direct that person to the ocean…and tell that person to jump.
- If you say "a lot" a lot, make sure you don't spell it "alot."
- If a person wishes you a "Happy New Years," ask which years.
- You shouldn't date anyone who wishes you a happy Valentime's Day...you just shouldn't.
- "Weather" is rain and sunshine and all that – "Whether" isn't.
- Your = possession/shows ownership | You're = contraction of "You are."
- There = place or idea | Their = possession/shows ownership | They're = contraction of They are.
- Its = possession/shows ownership | It's = contraction for It is or It has

Would you Mind vs. Would you: By now, we all know not to ask if a person *could* pass the salt. I'm sure people possess the ability to pass salt. If they didn't, you wouldn't be asking. If you're requesting something from someone, the polite way to ask is, "Will you please pass the salt?" Saying "would you mind" isn't asking them to do anything. It's simply checking to see if it would impose on them or not. You still have to follow up with your request. It's like asking someone if you can ask a question. Make it easier for all parties involved and just ask your question.

TEXT TALK: Text messaging tortures grammar. With the introduction of condensed communication (via technology), never has terrible grammar run more rampant. Reading incoming text is like trying to solve word scramble puzzles. Nobody has time for that! Your device likely has a spell-check, but it doesn't have a stupid-check. There's something satisfying about receiving a text message with correct grammar and punctuation. It's not necessary, but it says something about the sender. Unless you're between the ages of three and five years old, speaking in text message grammar in real life is a tragedy.

SLANG: Being a Gentlewoman is about being balanced enough to casually maneuver through all forms of society. She can speak the language of the land as well as the language of the culture and subculture. Stay connected to your roots and keep your ears to what's happening.

VULGARITY: There once was a time when a woman with a mouth full of foul language was consistent with a mouth full of fecal matter. It was considered "unladylike" for women to curse, while men were getting away with saying whatever we wanted. In the spirit of equality, I shun this notion. You have a choice. Self-expression is a vital component to being a gentlewoman, but I do challenge you to intellectually formulate thought without the constant use of indecent language. Vulgarity is generally reserved for unsophisticated thought. Refraining from cursing stretches the mind to create and express ideas more fluidly. With obscenities in vogue, a Lady who speaks and writes well is an unexpected yet welcomed kiss from a crush—rare and delightful.

CONVERSATION: The measure of a great conversationalist is how well she listens. Don't just talk to hear yourself speak, but speak to learn. Only a fool knows she knows it all. It's perfectly OK to excuse yourself at any time if you're on the receiving end of bad conversation. Don't correct a stranger who mispronounces a word, instead use the word correctly in your response and that person will get the point. Feel free to correct family and friends in private, not in the company of others. No matter how great the temptation, don't finish someone's sentence for her/him. It can make the speaker feel pathetic. Try to avoid the use of filler words such as "uh," "like" and "you know what I'm saying." It's perfectly okay to stop and think about your next thought. When you begin and end a sentence with, "You know what I'm saying," we don't know what you're saying. Be clear. Be concise. Refrain from being verbose by making valid points in few words. If you must expound on a topic, do so by gaging the level of attentiveness from your listener(s). If your audience displays signs of disinterest, it's time for you to wrap it up. If your audience is attentive, show them your intellect by making thought-provoking points while still exercising brevity.

A great piece of advice is to know a little about a lot! Or you can know a lot about a little. Both come with their advantages and disadvantages. I've laid some of them on the next page. Decide what's best for you.

Know a little about a lot

PROS
-Advantages in business
-Cultural/societal awareness
-Conversational in current
global affairs

CONS
-Artificial sophistication /
Superficial sound bites
-No depth
-Can easily be exposed

HOW
-Read online articles
-Tune into the news

PROS
-Authentic knowledge base
-In-depth information
-Able to teach others new
thoughts & ideas

CONS
-Tends to be verbose
-Limited mainstream
knowledge
-Minimal engagement

HOW
-Read books
-Take a class

Know a lot about a little

The Caution of Words

"We are the masters of the unsaid words, but slaves of those we let slip out." -**Winston Churchill**

It's wise to think about what you think about because thoughts become things. Sounds strange, I know, but there's truly an uncanny power in words. When my siblings were younger, my dad would always pour words of love and confirmation into us. He was, and still is very intentional about how he speaks to his family. Every word my father has put into us has come out of us. I've understood the power in words for a long time.

The average person knows 12,000-20,000 of them. When you filter through your arsenal, be mindful of what you choose to say because your words are either poison or fruit. When you speak, your mind and spirit agree, and things are set in motion. The *Man Upstairs* said let there be light and there was light. The universe was spoken into existence. You were made in His image.

Be wise about the music you let in and the words being spoken that you recite. You might be confirming some of those very things in your life. Don't be careless with your lexicon. Be slower to speak and quicker to think. When expressing yourself, what are you really trying to convey? Instead of referring to something incredible as "unbelievable," state that you're in awe of how amazing God is and how He shows up when you least expect it. Say what you mean and mean what you say. Be intentional about your word choices. Speak about what God's promises are at all times. Speak it into your career, your finances, your home, your relationships and your family.

Communication Killed Assumption

In Today's News, Assumption was Found Dead and Communication has been Arrested in Connection with the Murder

The miscommunication of men and women has led to debate, divorce and death. Our understanding of each other is only half the battle. Communication with the opposite sex is like trying to send a text message with a cell phone on an international flight – you attempt delivery, but it just won't go through. The main problem with a lack of effective communication is that it forces folks to jump to their own conclusions.

When we say, "You look pretty today," you might hear, "Yesterday you were ugly–and each day before then, too." When you say, "Who's that calling?" we can possibly hear, "Are you cheating on me?" When we smile and say, "Good morning," to a stranger, she might hear, "I like you, I want you, let's have sex." Oh, what a wonderful world!

The bottom line is most Ladies want to know the way men think. They'd like to know why we have double standards, why we lie and lead them on, why we're not upfront, why we're so afraid to commit, why we don't completely answer questions, why we have a hard time communicating and when there will be an answer to all of these damn questions. When men refuse to address the issues, women begin to assume the answers. Some of you think a few dinner dates and some intimacy makes a man your boyfriend, while the man is simply enjoying your company. You then begin to expect much more than your date is willing to offer because you're communicating two totally different things.

That's the problem that most men have with women today. We simply don't understand how "yes" can mean "no" and why "nothing is wrong" means something is definitely wrong, and it needs to be addressed not now, but right now. When you say, "Just kidding," you're telling the damn truth. When you point out something sweet another man does, you want us to do it too–but we must do it better. Telling you you're acting crazy is the worst way to get you to stop acting crazy. If you look upset, you're upset and mad at us for us not knowing why you're mad at us. If you ask, "Is that what you're wearing?" you probably want us to change. Sometimes you push us away to see if we're willing to come forward. If you leave upset, are we supposed to follow you? When you cry it's best to hold you tight and not say a word. You test our reactions, observe and judge our every action, expression, word and gesture. You might notice how long it takes us to respond to a text message and analyze why it took that long.

Let us know that you create a connection and sense of intimacy through communication and your personal questions aren't intended to invade our privacy. That way we'll stop texting, and start calling. That way we won't be so afraid to open up. A great start to opening up is to get us to actually answer your questions. In order to facilitate this, try sharing personal stories we can relate to and encourage us to share some of our own. Follow up with intriguing inquiries that don't initially feel invasive. This isn't about handholding and babysitting us through a process. It's about being an adult and communicating to be understood. A woman puts into a relationship exactly what she expects out of it. Partnerships are useless with no connection. Communication is cable, the remote, the receiver and sound system.

You really aren't as complicated as we make you out to be–you just want to be loved and express that much differently than we do. You view communication as intimacy. You desire to feel emotion from us. It's why you tell us about your day when we never asked, and don't feel like being bothered. Or when you ask us all sorts of detailed questions when we think it's unnecessary to be so specific. You communicate to dive into levels deeper than surface. To some of you, the mental stimulation is almost better than sex. To some of us, we'd just pick the sex.

Our communication barrier is so thick simply because men and women think and interpret information differently. In my experience, a woman's mind seems to respond more to emotion and empathy, whereas a man's mind generally responds to hard facts + reason. That's why when most of us talk we often choose "think," instead of "feel."

MAN: [*I _think_ that's unnecessary.*]

WOMAN: [*I _feel_ that's unnecessary.*]

MAN: [*I don't know what I _think_ about it.*]

WOMAN: [*I don't know how I _feel_ about it.*]

Whether it's a social construct or not, many women seem to be more nurturing than us. Ask a man to go to the store for bread and we'll bring back bread. Ask a woman to go to the store for bread and she'll bring back groceries. Not because she's wasting money– but because on the way out, she noticed the kid's cereal box was empty, the milk was low and there wasn't any dinner for Tuesday.

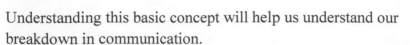

Understanding this basic concept will help us understand our breakdown in communication.

Some of us may be crazy, but we're not nuts and you damn sure can't crack us open. Ladies, never attempt to pry or force communication out of a man. The results are similar to prying out teeth, no anesthesia. Be more patient with us, love us harder and show us that we can count on you. If a man and a group of male friends watch TV in complete silence, they might feel they had a serious bonding moment. If a woman and her girlfriends watch TV in complete silence, something might be wrong. Understand that not all men connect through long talks. If we don't hound you with inquiries, it doesn't mean something's wrong – it probably means everything is right.

Don't ignore us and subsequently get mad at us ignoring you ignoring us. Half of the time, we don't know what's going on. This doesn't insinuate we don't care or we're not present in the relationship. It means we don't enjoy the guessing game. Genuine communication disturbs this type of silly behavior. Don't get upset with us, and then grow more upset with us for us not knowing why you're upset with us. Psychics aren't real, so either try learning the way we communicate or date a psychic. Good luck!

As simple as some of us seemingly are, we understand some ladies just don't understand us. Take a look at my "Five Communication Do's & Don'ts" to help you out:

Communication Do's:

1. **Do approach with caution**. The four words we hate to hear are "We need to talk." It's not what you say; it's how and when you say it.

2. **Do acknowledge our efforts**. A lot of men won't admit it, but we require affirmation just like you. So before you communicate that we're doing something wrong, acknowledge what we're doing right or even that you know we're trying. We want the same basic things you want. We desire love and we act out in crazy ways when we don't get it. We want affection and require the reassurance that we're doing things right. We want trust and companionship. Instead of shoes, we want sex. And you do, too. We want compliments and long, silent hugs when we've reached our limit. We all desire the same things.

3. **Do be upfront, but not "in your face upfront."** I know that sometimes women aren't blunt to protect a man's ego, but speak matter-of-factly so that we understand the serious tone and nature of the conversation. When we see that a woman is sure and clear about what she wants, we'll definitely straighten up and take notice. Most men like direct women because most men are direct, but there is truly an art to approaching us so that we not only receive what you're communicating, but also open up to you.

4. **Do find the right time we communicate together effectively**. Timing is everything. Sometimes an issue will arise that requires communication and since some women and men display emotion differently, she may want to discuss things in the heat of the moment. In the meantime, a logically driven man may want to sleep on it and discuss it when our mind is settled. You might not understand our

logical argument when you're arguing emotionally. Forcing communication while emotions are high is like sparking a lighter in a flammable gas factory. The best way to come to a compromise about finding the right time to effectively communicate is by communicating when nothing is wrong.

5. **Do speak in love and pick your battles**. Not everything under the sun needs to be communicated. Decide what's important and what can be figured out over time.

Communication Don'ts:

1. **Don't text him 10 times a day to ask over and over where the relationship is going**. You have to strike a healthy balance between letting a man know what you will and won't tolerate, while still allowing progression to happen naturally. We don't always go into situations looking for relationships, but we get into them because we recognize a good Lady when we see one. Forcing yourselves onto us creates a force around us that will block you. Set boundaries and state intentions early and you won't have to bring up "the talk" at all. We'll gladly do it for you.

2. **Don't *always* have something to say**. Sometimes communication is simply listening. Just as you need to vent, at times we need to vent and would like for you to just listen. Be there for us. We might not say it, but we need it.

3. **Don't communicate problems in public**. If you're out with friends and an issue occurs, keep your class and wait until you're behind closed doors to discuss it. Maintain your relationship's privacy and integrity because you'll eventually forget about your public blow-up, but friends

and family won't. Some of them will be happy to always remind you.

4. **Don't ignore body language**. Fifty-five percent of communication is non-verbal, thirty-eight percent is vocal (pitch, speed, volume, tone of voice) and only seven percent is actual words. So listen to what we do. If we've scheduled a time to talk about something and we look like we're not in the mood for discussion, but we made an effort to discuss anyway, just change the subject. It can wait.

5. **Don't focus on what we're not saying**. Forget what you'd like us to say, take us at face value. Most of the time our communication doesn't require an interpreter. As we understand that we're both saying the same thing, just saying it differently, then we can begin to move forward in understanding one another. Don't dive deep into shallow water.

Communication kills assumptions. The more we attempt to effectively communicate with each other, the more we can begin to properly love one another. Men and women desire the same thing – to be loved. It's the way in which we seek out love and attention that causes the friction. We may speak different dialects of the same language, but that's the beauty of it. Love is the language that a deaf woman can hear and a blind mind can see; it can be tasted without a tongue.

We must kill this senseless Venus vs. Mars act that's been going on for decades. We need you and you need us. It's not Venus vs. Mars, it's Venus with Mars. Let's focus on everything right with us, instead of everything wrong with us. Learn to appreciate, enjoy and love our differences instead of shunning them. That's what makes this life beautiful, and worth it. R.I.P. Assumptions.

Words say a little. Effort says a lot. Doing says it all.

Sometimes the King is a Woman

Sometimes the King is a Woman:
Independence Day

QUEEN

Look around. Sometimes there's just a Lady. At times there are no men to wear a crown.

Let's be honest about independence. Often it's something that happens to you, not a lifestyle choice. Maybe you were abandoned. Maybe you were left for dead. You have a responsibility to be truthful about it. Show your daughters the tears. Let them see you cry. Allow them to witness your pain. It can be dangerous for independent, strong women to maintain a brave face while putting themselves last, holding back tears and simultaneously holding everything together. It's dangerous because daughters are watching and daughters will become adults that mimic your behavior. They can carry the negativity that was rooted in your independence within their own lives. It's important to show them both sides of the story. Most kings get their heads cut off.

Sometimes independence is freedom, a necessary separation from a captor or pure self-reliance. It can turn out beautifully if you let it.

We claim women are becoming *too* independent, but who's responsible? What is too independent, anyway? When you can't rely on your significant other, you're insignificant to them and it's time for another. It seems men's duties are being outsourced. Are women slowly becoming the men they desire? You're beginning to step in for your fathers and for your relationships. Has it all gone too far?

Perhaps the advancement of women is a positive outcome due to the lack of chivalry from men. A Lady who doesn't depend on a man to change her tires, start her fires and kill her spiders is a Lady well equipped for the world. Learn all you need to learn to live. Basic survival skills don't depend on any man. An independent Lady knows no limits.

Powerful women only scare weak men

Turn down your worth for no one! Life is about balance and sometimes the experience is just better with the woman on top! Your independence doesn't need to be plastered on a t-shirt or thrown in our faces. Carry it with honor, but carry it with humility. If we're ever to get back to a place of community interdependence, you must walk lightly. Attempting to insult or emasculate a man by saying he's acting like a woman is a subconscious display of your own thoughts about yourself. It insinuates that you believe women are a weak sex. None of which is true, but you often subconsciously reinforce this patriarchal message and don't even know it. Think about the message you're sending.

In modern society, kings are people regarded as the finest and most important in their sphere. Sometimes the king is a woman. She's the presidential candidate and the CEO. She's the executive exercising etiquette in the office, then exercising at the gym on her lunch break. She understands that men aren't the sole cause of her problems and aren't the answer to her problems, either. She

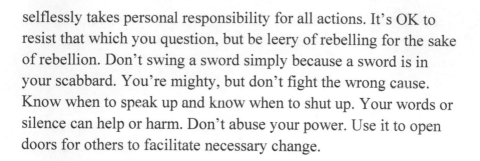

selflessly takes personal responsibility for all actions. It's OK to resist that which you question, but be leery of rebelling for the sake of rebellion. Don't swing a sword simply because a sword is in your scabbard. You're mighty, but don't fight the wrong cause. Know when to speak up and know when to shut up. Your words or silence can help or harm. Don't abuse your power. Use it to open doors for others to facilitate necessary change.

Don't let her independence fool you...she still wants to be courted

You might be single, secure and satisfied, but sometimes you just want to go out on a cool date and be treated like a Lady. As independent as some women are, they adore chivalry. Life isn't supposed to be lived without us. The world is a colder place without men of valor. Chivalry is that scarf when you didn't realize how unforgiving London winters can be–you might think you're good without it, but you surely appreciate it when it's there.

The "S" Word

Don't be scared of submission or scared into submission. I wish couples understood the "S" word isn't a curse. The problem with the word is that it brings back bad memories of improper usage and triggers negative emotions. Historically, women submitted to men in ways that weren't honorable. Submission is equated to loss of power. Why would women want to give up what they've worked so hard to gain? Submission requires yielding, humility and a partner. Something about that recipe sounds like a disaster to most.

Men and women should both submit to each other. Men must yield to their wives as well. Most of us conveniently leave that part out. Submission is intended for marital relationships where each partner is required to daily die of self and surrender to one another. Marriage requires balance that involves giving in to your partner for the betterment of the union. All thoughts, opinions and decisions matter in marriage. You should only want someone you're willing to submit to. Why would you marry someone whose direction you don't trust? I question your ability to properly select a mate if you can't submit to your mate.

Having testicles doesn't automatically make us leaders. When our words match our efforts and our results, then we deserve your trust. You'll respect our leadership when you trust our leadership. The key is being with the right man to submit to.

It's not about dictatorship, control and obeying him simply because he's a man–it's about respecting your home. That doesn't mean a woman has no rights in the home, or is unable to make decisions. It's about taking turns guiding your relationship.

I know not a powerful man who wasn't influenced, inspired or empowered by a wonderful woman? A wise man always seeks his Lady's counsel. A president's greatest advisor is his wife because *alongside* any great man stands a powerful Lady. Who can we depend on to always be there? Who do we call for encouragement? A woman with an opinion is the relief of ice on a back on a scorching summer night. Women have had our backs since the beginning--it's about time to return the favor.
Never forget: After God, there's you. Long Live the King!

Wear your crown.

Victoria's Secret

Victoria's Secret: *Essence of Elegance*

There's just something about Victoria. Her majesty's ascension to the throne began in 1837, lasting for 63 years and 216 days. Her reign as queen is the longest in British history. The regal four-wheeled horse-drawn carriage with a collapsible hood was named after her. The capitals of Seychelles and British Columbia both bare her moniker. Her name flows through the largest lake in Africa, drops from a waterfall in Zimbabwe and hangs from a mountain peak in Hong Kong. In Canada, she maintains a national holiday in her glory celebrated every May 24th. There have been several queens pre-Victoria and post-Victoria, but her name carries a legacy that remains present.

What is it about this Victoria?

Victoria's secret is much more than lingerie.

Her name has become an adjective that boasts an era of elegance. The Victorian Era was a period of values characterized by an intense conviction for morals and etiquette. Additionally, architecture, decorative arts and fashion became synonymous with the times. The era was culturally aware. It was interested in literature, theater, the opera and music. Gentlemen attended dining clubs similar to today. Industrial communication links even improved through the advancement of technology and engineering. If only the queen's prowess could have linked the man vs. woman communication gap in the process. But don't let the sophisticated nature of the era fool you. Classicism diminished as the culture created communal and inclusive social values. Though elegant charm and refinement were ever-present, the beauty of all cultures

139

weren't just tolerated – they were embraced. What beauty, this Victorian era! The queen's elegance alone influenced an entire society to prosper. In the abridged philosophical words, "No one woman should have all that power." Oh, but she does. All women do.

Victoria's secret was about elegance, while *Victoria's Secret* is about euphemistic eroticism. In the late 19th century, these two worlds couldn't co-exist. Feminine sexuality was looked down upon as a threat that could undermine you. Most people wouldn't take you seriously and you'd have to work that much harder to prove yourself. But today's gentlewoman can be both sexy and elegant without compromising her integrity, her values or herself. The gentlewoman may have some traditional values, but she's indeed a modern Lady. We've grown from that era. Despite what society suggests, a Lady has freedom to be exactly who she is. She has a keen awareness and control over her sensuality. Sex doesn't define her – it's a part of culture and a part of life. Don't be afraid to be sexy. A gentlewoman always knows when not to be so gentle.

People are drawn to a Lady's ability to diversify her interests. There's something sexy about a Lady who can digest *Reader's Digest* while maintaining a subscription to *Maxim*. Or can go from *The New Yorker* to *ESSENCE* Magazine without a whimper. She has mass taste. We appreciate a Lady who engages in intellectual banter while sipping a cold beer – a dichotomy for the ages. One ankle gracefully crosses the other preventing her soul from being exposed. Everything about her says class, but past the undetectable eye rests permanent ink above her spine, hidden by hair that spills down her neck like excess champagne. Only the perfect suitor can see past the obvious. He fully understands that there's nothing sexier than realizing beneath her business acumen and poise stands a Lady with very little inhibition.

What a beautiful juxtaposition: A Lady in the streets, but someone entirely less graceful in the bedroom with her husband. Some consider it to be the best of both worlds, like having wine while watching a sunset – you're intoxicated by the taste of the juices, yet sobered by nature's beauty. The more important message the mantra suggests is being you without apology, but having discernment and exercising safety. We gush about a Lady who looks like a model, but doesn't act like a stereotypical one. We adore a gentlewoman who takes control in the corporate world, but relinquishes it on the weekends with her husband. That balance is beautiful.

Laurel Thatcher Ulrich once said, "**Well-behaved women rarely make history**." For far too long, women have been persecuted for having the same desires as men. Women possess clever contrasts just like we do and it's about time they freely express them however they desire without persecution. It's time to cancel our subscription to contradictions. The classiest Lady might still want her hair pulled…pardon my French.

While it's true that many men prefer a Lady with an edge, we don't want her falling off the edge. Life is a balancing act. We want to be able to bring you home to mom, marry you and turn you into a mom. Be authentically you and still make history.

Of course, plenty of people enjoy the predictability of a classy Lady who knows all the right things to say and do. But what's more attractive is when you display the unpredictable you. Never underestimate the Lady bold enough to be her.

A man must charm, convince and sometimes deceive his way into power. A silent woman can influence a nation. Jacqueline Kennedy Onassis was photographed in cropped pants on the Italian isle of Capri. Those pants came to be known as capris. Whether covered up or hardly covered at all, your essence of elegance will forever shine through.

Legacies aren't limited to royalty. It's important to lead a life that says, "I was here and I did it my way."

The Victorian way.

The gentlewoman way.

Here's your crown.

Interlude
Cease and Desist

Cease and Desist: Quit
Certified Mail

To Whom It May Concern:

I am writing on behalf of everyone to notify you of your illegal behavior. It has come to our attention that you began to use the name "Gentlewoman." We interpret this action as an effort by you to confuse who you are with the contents of this book of the same name.

The use of the "Gentlewoman" name is unauthorized and is likely to cause confusion, mistake or to deceive the public and may be a violation of the federally protected rights. Your use of "Gentlewoman" falsely creates the impression that the contents of this book are associated or affiliated with your behavior.

We demand that you immediately:
Quit saying, "All men are the same," and start saying, "I date the same type of men." Quit showing up with a full face of make up just to fake sweat at the gym. Quit posting photos from the neck up pretending to be slim. The cut and paste isn't a workout and Photoshop isn't a gym. Quit bleaching your beautiful face attempting to pass as light-skinned. Quit fronting with a lace-front and just let your natural hair win. Quit focusing on all that's shallow and ignoring your beauty within. Fake hair, fake breasts, fake nails, injected lips, but you only demand real men?

We demand that you immediately inform men:
Quit acting like you're interested. You chase me until I give in. Then after the unprotected sex, you say you just want to be friends.

Quit calling me crazy. You weren't saying all that back when. You said I was cool; you said I was the one; you caused me to change within. Quit acting like this baby isn't yours. Quit saying I've been with other men. Quit blaming this all on your father – you're an adult, he left when you were ten. Quit saying you're a grown ass man, yet you neglect the responsibilities of grown ass men. Quit blaming this all on karma. Karma's only a bitch if you are, my friend.

We demand that everyone immediately:
Quit all these contradictions. Quit giving up on each other on a whim. We're at war acting like we don't need each other, when women are what we need in this life of sin. Let's quit the Venus versus Mars talk. Let's quit thinking there's always something to defend. Let's take greater strides; let's swallow our pride. Man needs woman, and she needs him.

Progression comes with time and awareness. If you're old enough to read these words, you're old enough to change. Don't take my words so literally. Just take the message and omit the messenger's wit. Although you're starting anew and beginning again, some of you just need to quit.

If you don't comply with these cease and desist demands, please be advised that legal action will be pursued. Before taking these steps, however, I wish to give you one opportunity to discontinue your conduct. Please sign below and continue reading.

Sincerely,
Everyone

X_____ (your signature)

145

Untitled

Untitled: ...

Beyond confidence, underneath the eyes and over many heads, a woman's mystique is indefinable. It triggers, but doesn't satisfy the human senses. You can't hear it, see it, smell it, taste it or touch it, but you can feel it, certainly. A woman's presence is a force that forces the nervous system to respond. It evokes detailed reactions: Perspiration drips from those unprepared for its splendor. Confidence evaporates from the heat of her existence. Our once-so-sure self is faced with newfound uncertainty. Her sensation causes us to question everything we once knew to be true:

"Is my tie straight?" "Do I look OK?" "Does my breath stink?"

No shadow exists, but you can perceive it. The temperature in the room changes and you know it when it's there. You know when a Lady has arrived!

It's powerful. It stirs emotion and generates confusion. Those unwilling to accept her splendor settle for envy. It creates chaos and evokes fear. She's luxury. She's simplicity. She talks the talk, and walks the walk. Confidence courts her and she sleeps with peace of mind…but she's not kissing and telling. Those afraid call her bitch. Those aware call her gentlewoman.

We've tried to apply suitable adjectives for your description. The injustice of each word fails miserably. A woman is made up of beautiful contrasts and clever contradictions. People try to slap a label on you and all that you do. I tried to capture your essence in this book, but your spirit is free. Your beauty can't be contained. Simply put, you're untitled.

Gentlewoman

Gentlewoman: *Class is Back in Session*
Essentials for a Lady

God gave you an empty **canvas** *and provided the paint and the brush. It's up to you to fill your canvas with vivid colors, painting a captivating* **picture**.

Power in Colors

-**Black** *is classic, stylish and timeless. It's the color of power. It's dominant and has the ability to drown out any of its predecessors. It's the color of choice in fashion and it appears to make one look thinner.*

-**White** *is elegant. It's the color of purity and innocence. It's light, neutral and goes with everything.*

-**Red** *is considered a power color that commands attention. It's very passionate intense and sexy. It's the color of love.*

-**Blue** *is a dominant yet peaceful color. It's calming and represents peace and loyalty.*

-**Green** *is refreshing, relaxing and easy on the eye. It's a*

*favorable color in décor and
represents masculinity and
wealth.*

*-**Yellow** is a bold and sexy
attention-getter. As the color
of happiness and hope, it
enhances concentration and
focus. When paired with
gray, magic happens!*

*-**Purple** is a regal color of
kings and queens alike. It's a
color of honor and
sophistication.*

*-**Brown** is a masculine color.
As the color of oak, it's
reliable and genuine.*

*Each color unique in its own
right, paired with the right
combination, can create an
unimaginable experience.*

The beauty of the world lies in its diverse collection of cultures,
experiences and differences. It's essential for the gentlewoman to
embrace these distinctive collections, thus providing the option to
add to and enhance her own lifestyle. Possessing these pleasingly
varied abilities makes you a well-rounded woman. That fine
balance is beyond beautiful.

But balance isn't an art form achieved from sunrise to sunset. It
requires practice and consistency, like any new concept that the
brain attempts to soak up and make habit. This chapter provides a

guiding principle in matters of artistic beauty and taste. Let's considerately assume you know not a thing about anything. This approach will provide the basic essentials that need to be in every woman's possession—that is if you strive to be an appealing Lady of eclectic aesthetics, providing delight in appearance or manner. I'm speaking to the gentlewoman who strives to be confident, bold and timeless without thought.

   "Intelligent people are always open to new ideas. In fact, they look for them."
~~Proverbs 18:15

MORNINGS.

You're still here. You still have a purpose. Mornings are a beautiful reminder of that. Stop what you're doing, close your eyes, hear yourself breathe and say thank you. Focus and allow your joy to flow. Let your mind be at ease and get your clarity. Do this daily.

PREPARATION.

There's an art to getting ready that requires comfort. For some, this is a ceremonial process. Let music accompany you on your journey or turn on some talk radio. What's your soundtrack to getting ready? Grab your playlist and prepare to love on yourself. Wait, not like that. You know what I mean.

Prep-time: 1 - 3 hours for the average healthy Lady on an average day.

-**The Wardrobe:** Why is this first on the list? Because it cuts down on time and leaves room for what's more important. Pick out and prepare your clothes a day in advance. You can even pick out your wardrobe for the entire week at the start of the week. It's no different than the selection process you go through when deciding which clothes to pack for a vacation. This might pose a problem for the stylish gentlewoman who selects her clothing in the moment according to how she's feeling. All others can attempt this format for time's sake. Get to a point where getting dressed in the morning should require the least amount of thought in your day! Style is effortless.

-The Meal: See *Shut Up & Train* chapter.

-The Exercise: See *Shut Up & Train* chapter.

-The Hygiene: If cleanliness is next to Godliness, then a toothbrush needs to be next to your mouth. I've enlisted the advice of "Turning Natural" CEO, Jerri Evans for further explanation: *The majority of us brush our teeth at least twice a day, however, hardly recognize that little warning label that says, "If swallowed contact poison control immediately." First, why would you put anything in your mouth that requires you to contact a poison control center if ingested? No, one time of not properly rinsing your mouth out after brushing will send you to the hospital, but think about how many times in your life you have and will brush your teeth? Is that a risk you're willing to take? Try natural toothpaste, something fluoride and chemical free like Neem Toothpaste, an excellent anti-bacterial component. Need a quick teeth whitener without the pricy dental bill or nasty chemical filled strips? Try baking soda and peroxide! It's quick, natural and it works!*

-The Shower: Some view the shower as a sanctuary; a sacred place to relax, release and get some necessary *me* time. Others view the shower as a place to quickly wash their rear and get on with their day. Whichever way you see it, go ahead and brush your teeth before you get in or bring the toothpaste/toothbrush in with you. Bad breath is bad etiquette. A refusal to scrape your tongue and chew some gum is a threat to society. You can't be cute with bad breath. You and your breath should match. Be sure to wash in all places susceptible to odor. There's nothing more useless than exiting a shower smelling the same way you entered.

-The Bathing: Baths are traditionally synonymous with relaxation and pampering. A gentlewoman might slip off a silk slip and slip into a hot bath as her form disappears into foam. Wine and candles are likely to join her on the journey. Make sure a few glasses of water are readily available as well. Dehydration can occur rapidly. But don't allow that to stress you out. Bathing is therapeutic. It relaxes your muscles, calms your mind, helps clear the system of toxins, moisturizes with added natural oils, stimulates circulation and clears your lymph system whilst you sit back, breath deeply and daydream. Visits to your bath can reduce visits to your doctor. Hot water in tubs assists in maintaining muscle position and equal tension on the skeletal system. Baths can also help reduce cramps and tension headaches. As exquisite as this all is, you're going to need to stand up and rinse yourself off. Bathing is beautiful, but befouling.

-The Makeup: As men, we won't understand everything you do and that's OK. We'll never understand why some of you shave your eyebrows off only to immediately draw them back on. Some of you look permanently surprised. Well, so are we. But we also understand that makeup is an art and there's a method to the application.

I've enlisted the help of television news anchor and former makeup artist veteran Letisha Bereola to explain *what the everyday women should know about makeup*:

Letisha Bereola
News Anchor | Reporter | Former Makeup Artist

There are a few misconceptions out there, but let's tackle the "cake face" myth. I'd often find women who'd shy away from makeup because they didn't want to look "fake" or appear to have makeup on. Makeup doesn't have to look heavy! When your skin is moisturized, primed and ready for application, the makeup can help you achieve a healthy glow. Don't let someone else's bad makeup application scare you away from experimenting for yourself. You have control over what you use and how you use it.

What should every woman know about makeup?
It's intended to highlight existing beauty, not make you beautiful. Makeup is supposed to bring out your best, even when you might not feel your best. You can highlight and conceal, add color or go nude. However you feel on any given day, makeup can help achieve the look to match your mood. Similar to your fashion and your hairstyle, your makeup allows you to try something new and fresh. It's also a great tool for you to explore different looks on yourself. The best part is it comes right off if you're not feeling it!

What should every woman have in her makeup bag?
A good mascara! Those days when you're in a rush, hop in the car and take a peek into the rear view mirror – mascara will help tired eyes open right up. Pack a good gloss to touch up your lips after lunch. Also, throw in blot films or powder to help bring down shine after a long day.

What should be avoided?

Makeup is a very personal choice. Just avoid settling for less. If you haven't found the perfect foundation, keep trying. Ask for samples until you find what you love. And avoid getting into a makeup rut. You're beautiful in more than one shade of lipstick or eye shadow. Try new things! You'll be surprised at where your curiosity will take you.

Makeup tips and tricks:

Keep your brows in shape. You'll find it easier to apply eye makeup when that arch is just right. Also, learn how to contour and highlight your face. It's a fun process to see how your face adapts to this simple technique.

What is some final advice?

I'm a big advocate of finding a makeup artist that you can trust. They're in your local malls and boutiques waiting for women like you. It can take a few tries, but once you find one (or even two from different brands), that artist will help make your makeup journey fun and informative. A good artist keeps you up-to-date on the latest trends, helps you take care of your skin and introduces you to the latest products. For those big life moments, there's nothing better than calling someone you can trust to help you look and feel your best!

Letisha Bereola is a News Anchor | Reporter | Journalist | Former Makeup Artist

-**The Hair:** A woman's hair is often considered a sense of pride. For some, it's a symbolic connection to femininity more sacred than we realize. I used to hate weaves. I felt the nation's economy could be fixed if we got rid of them. When running my fingers

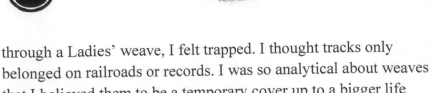

through a Ladies' weave, I felt trapped. I thought tracks only belonged on railroads or records. I was so analytical about weaves that I believed them to be a temporary cover up to a bigger life issue. I was so anti-weave that I would search for tracks like a producer – and if I located one, the party was over!

"I remember when I used to talk trash about women who wore weaves, feeling superior to them. Then I got one...&
I shut the hell up." **–Gabrielle Union**

I think the problem most men have with weave is that it looks like weave. If you can't afford to keep it up, take it out. The men I polled suggested that if they couldn't tell, oh, what the hell. Some men don't seem to care as long as it looks like her hair. They don't like for it to be too much and hate it if it's unable to be touched. Many men claim they prefer a Lady natural, but constantly pass up the woman with a natural. Some men even said that weave implies a woman is lazy. My response is simple: Some of your own mothers who raised badass children like you while holding down two or more jobs wore *convenient* weaves. Are you calling them lazy? Besides, wearing a ball cap is just as *lazy*. Some men even said, "God didn't make women with weave–it's unnatural." He didn't, but He did create women with personalities and a desire to be expressive. And he didn't create you to rule over women.

However, some men support a Lady doing whatever she wants to do to feel beautiful. One person surveyed said, "Weave is fine. Any enhancement works as long as she's not self-conscious of her natural beauty and doesn't overdo it." My response is that if she wants to "over-do" it, she can. Why? Well, because it's her hair. However, one person polled made a great observation by suggestion that most *weavy* women he's come in contact with are

156

very standoffish about their hair. When it's time to get intimate, her hair is off limits. Some women like their hair pulled…as long as it can't be pulled off. The most sensible response was, "Personally, I don't care. I have more things to worry about, like can she hold an interesting conversation." What's in her heard is always more important than what's on it.

In my own experience with women, I've come to learn that weaves, extensions, wigs and what women chose to do with their hair has nothing to do with me and my opinion. No woman other than my mother has ever had input on my hair, so why should men have input in what a woman decides to do with her hair? Weaves don't conclude anything. Like a purse, manicured nails or sexy shoes, a weave is simply an accessory. Sometimes a woman's decision is as simple as, "I wonder what I'd look like with short hair, but don't want to cut it." Or, "I wonder what my hair would look like blonde without my having to dye and damage it." It's a fun and creative way to experiment with hair. No woman should be penalized for discovering herself. If weave is done correctly and maintained, weave can promote healthy hair by giving it a break. It took this kind of understanding for me to give ladies' hair a break.

But your hair should never determine your quality of life. If you can't jump in a swimming pool when you want, kiss in the rain or sweat in a gym, you're not fully living. Let your weave help you, not hinder you. Some women do in fact let their hair define them. If you fall victim to this trap, your self-esteem becomes a contingency. To let your worth be determined by what's on your head and not what's in it is a tragedy. Take into consideration what your man likes and dislikes, but ultimately do what makes you satisfied. Be as comfortable, confident and sexy with or without weave.

Gentlemen reading, this is for you: Most of your celebrity crushes and thousands of beautiful women sport weaves. Are they suddenly undesirable because of this? We have every right to not want to date a woman with weave because it's a simple matter of preference. But to go as far as labeling women or making assumptions about their security and how they view themselves is way off base. Your mom probably wears weave and your grandma might own two wigs. Don't for one moment pretend to be the greater gender – if you're driving a friend's car like it's yours don't worry about her hair and if it's hers. Unless you're her hairdresser, stay the hell out of her head.

Us men may never fully understand why some women decide to place hair from India or Brazil inside of their head and let it simmer for one to two months. Perhaps it's not for us to understand. Men do men things and women do women things. Not everything is to be understood by everyone because not everything is for everybody. But all must understand one thing – weaves have expiration dates!
The reality is not every woman experiences hair the same way. Some will experience hair loss to aging, stress, genetics, hormones and more. Various hair chemicals can also cause increased breakage that lead to hair loss. Then there's chemotherapy, alopecia, lupus and more. Without hair, you still wear your crown. You're still 100 percent woman.

GROOMING.
A Lady's true organization is commonly revealed in her home. If you don't keep your bathroom clean, some would assume you don't keep your *back room* clean.

Body Hair: In western society, many women consider it appropriate to have the hair on their legs and armpits shaved. If you decide to keep it, be sure to treat it. You're the boss, but your body hair is like an employee – manage it! All human hair requires maintenance to maintain its health. If you're in a relationship and care about the opinion of your significant other, ask your lover's opinion. If body hair doesn't turn your love on, maybe it's time to mow the lawn. It's your body, your choice.

Antiperspirant/Deodorant: When wearing dark tops with sleeves, use clear deodorant. Avoid white bars as they may leave residue on your garment. To avoid possible stains altogether, use products that don't contain aluminum. When aluminum and perspiration mix, it can cause discoloration on your clothing. According to Jeri Evans, *antiperspirant deodorants are another daily used item that is overlooked, but overtime can become harmful. Where does the sweat go if it doesn't come out of the pores it's supposed to come out of? Well Ladies, you may smell like a summer linen's breeze, but sweating is actually your body's way of helping to keep your skin clean. Everyday, toxins build up in your pores that need to be released—when they're not, they re-enter the body throwing the lymphatic system out of whack. More women are contracting breast cancer rooting from the lymph nodes under the arm more than ever before. When shopping for deodorants look for aluminum free products. As an option, try crystal deodorant—it's fragrant and aluminum free. If you just absolutely need fragrance, add your favorite essential oil.*

The Skin You're In: Evans has this to say:
Now flawless skin is a thing of beauty. We coddle it, we nourish it and we try to improve it. Yet, we regularly dis it as "only" skin. It's misunderstood and undervalued. Oily, rough, dry, blemished,

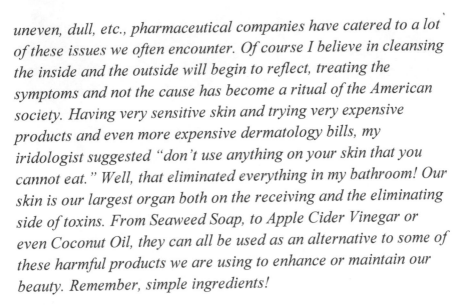

uneven, dull, etc., pharmaceutical companies have catered to a lot of these issues we often encounter. Of course I believe in cleansing the inside and the outside will begin to reflect, treating the symptoms and not the cause has become a ritual of the American society. Having very sensitive skin and trying very expensive products and even more expensive dermatology bills, my iridologist suggested "don't use anything on your skin that you cannot eat." Well, that eliminated everything in my bathroom! Our skin is our largest organ both on the receiving and the eliminating side of toxins. From Seaweed Soap, to Apple Cider Vinegar or even Coconut Oil, they can all be used as an alternative to some of these harmful products we are using to enhance or maintain our beauty. Remember, simple ingredients!

Jerri Evans is the CEO of Turning Natural, a Juice Bar in Washington, D.C. where she provides detoxes & juice cleanses | turningnatural.com

SITTING.

There's no need to balance a book on your head to check your posture. Put books in your head, not on your head. It's not just about sitting pretty. Good posture isn't just for the aesthetics – it can prevent health issues. It helps contribute to the normal functioning of the nervous system. Your posture doesn't only reflect, but also affects your mood. Carrying the body in a more upright position can improve mood and energy levels, while slouching can make you feel less energetic and more depressed. Some of your neck or back problems and even headaches are a result of bad posture. All that time spent looking at your cell phone screen can affect you. Head up, shoulders back and stomach in. Sit at a chair with firm low back support and stretch every hour if you sit for long periods of time. Remove bulky items (phone, wallet, candy, etc.) from your back pocket because it can cause a hip imbalance. If you're at a desk, sit erect and adjust the chair to ensure your elbows are desk-level. You can even use a footrest to keep pressure off the back of your legs.

Unless you want your legs to be the focal point of an encounter, sit with them together and crossed at the ankles. If you're wearing a short skirt with your legs crossed, most men won't mind the preview, but it's distracting and revealing–especially if you don't prefer panties. When wearing trousers or longer fabrics, feel free to cross at the knees.

Sometimes your outfit will disagree with you sitting down. Traditionally, a gentleman offers his seat to a gentlewoman when all other seats in the area are occupied. Nowadays, this gesture is mainly for pregnant women, women with children, the elderly and/or the disabled. It's a kind gesture not to be taken offensively. If you prefer to stand, simply say, "I'm fine, thank you."

Don't hesitate to return the gesture. If you're sitting in a public place and notice an elderly woman or man who needs a seat, be generous enough to offer yours to that person. The same goes for the disabled or anyone you feel could use the convenience of a seat more than you. Most people will probably be surprised by your willingness to exercise etiquette and thank you tremendously. If you're in a busy city like New York or London, your little labor of love will be spread throughout the heart of the city. Good behavior is contagious. Pass it on!

COOL.

Femininity is the art of being a Lady. It's sexy. It's in your energy
and confidence, not just appearance–that's why you receive all
those compliments on your *worst* day. It's the way a sundress
flows just enough to be respectable, but audacious enough to
display those curves. You can be fully dressed in a room full of
little black dresses and by far be the sexiest in the room. Don't get
me wrong; we certainly think the short dresses are sexy, but a
classy Lady drains the attention in any room.

THE LESS YOU REVEAL, THE MORE WE WONDER.

Even prostitutes used to dress with class. They got paid for every layer of clothing they took off. But on our quest to becoming a progressive and advanced society, lines in the sand got covered.

A gentlewoman's appeal isn't dependent upon threads and fabrics. In college, I had the biggest crush on a young Lady who wasn't physically the ideal "type." But every Wednesday around 12:14PM, she'd stride into the cafeteria in gym clothes sucking the room dry of all the attention. She was aware of her effect, but too cool to care. What was her intangible appeal that had my attention?

"Style is a simple way of saying complicated things." -Jean Cocteau

I've enlisted the help of international celebrity wardrobe and fashion stylist Toye Adedipe for the details:

Toye Adedipe
Celebrity Wardrobe & Fashion Stylist | Designer | Artist

In college, I was exposed to the retail side of fashion through modeling. It intrigued me how people made a living off of selling clothing. I came across a motivating article of a woman who was a famous fashion stylist in L.A. Did my research, gave her a call and developed an authentic relationship that lead to an internship. This taught me work ethic, but also taught me that I wasn't assistant material. However, it increased my drive and determination to command to the universe that I was going to become a fashion stylist and do things my way. I didn't know how I was going to do it, but I knew I was capable of doing it. I had to honor that and prove it to myself. That lead me to a road where I was able to accomplish everything in the industry that I wanted to accomplish. But I still needed to decide if my passion and drive to prove people wrong were balanced. I finally figured out it's not about other people, it's about me. The passion is there. I'm proving it to myself. I hope my honesty can help you overcome your own challenges.

What are the basics every gentlewoman should have?
First let me say this: Anyone can be fashionable, but to have style, you must hone in on the building blocks of what makes you great and unique. Now, the basics are:

1. *A Durable Bra.*
2. *Spanx.*
3. *Strapless Bra.*
4. *A Little Black Dress. It's timeless, classic and can take you through many generations.*
5. *Black + Nude Pumps. It's just a no-brainer.*
6. *Good Pair of Heels (open or closed toe).*
7. *Red Lipstick.*
8. *Small Set of Pearl Earrings. They're just classic.*
9. *Good Set of Golden Hoop Earrings. No matter your skin tone, religion or background, it's something that can play to the masses.*
10. *Classic Cut Dark Denim Jeans. No matter your size. Most women I dress are conscious about their butts. Whether they want it to look smaller or bigger, the one consistency is they want it to look good. One of the keys to a good-looking butt is finding a jean that has impeccable pocket placement. Always try to find back pockets that rest right at*

the middle of your butt and continue downward. This makes the waist look smaller and longer and the butt look higher and firmer. The front pockets should hit your hip, not your waist. If you're a hippy woman and the jean pocket is too high, it makes you look disproportionate. Cuts can change the dynamic of a body. It's important to have a strong construction of denim that's comfortable, but also makes you look good.

When dressing a woman, the first thing I try to hone in on is your physical strength(s) and what's naturally part of your aesthetics. It could be your lips, eyes or skin tone. It could be your long legs and torso. Maybe it's the fact that you're shorter and you can get away with wearing the six-inch heels that tall women won't wear in fear of appearing too exaggerated. Maybe you have a bed of hair that's curly or naturally kinky and beautiful and strong – you can incorporate that into your accessories. Pick out a certain color that works for you and your hair or accessories that work best for your hair. It can be a flower or even a jewel. It's a statement that confidently says: One of my features is the fact that I have really great, cool hair...just in case you didn't know! Find the balance of your strengths and then play up on them.

Don't be afraid to take the influence of somebody and say, I can identify with how she did it – now this is how I'm going to make it work for me.

What are some ways any woman can look her best in her clothes?

Two dichotomies are happening where women are being told to be a smaller size, but on the other side of the spectrum, women are being told it's better to have curves with a big butt and big boobs.

165

Just be you, but be healthy. If you desire curves, but you're thinner, find what clothing works for you as a woman to accentuate your own curves. Maybe go for a peplum top or jeans with a pattern or print that make your bottom portion look curvier and fuller. Some call it manipulating the eye, but I call it honing in on the features that you want to stand out.

You must create a foundation before building a home. Undergarments are great for smoothing out and creating a seamless line.

A strong basic heel / pump elongates you, makes you stand taller, creates a better posture and supplements the energy when you walk into a room that says: I'm here!

But a true, grounded style comes from within. It's a spiritual thing. Style is a catalyst. It's an exclamation point of what's already in you.

Let's end the myth! Who do women dress for?
There's an unfortunate competitive streak that occurs within the realm of Hollywood and some of the Lady clients I might work with. They're adamant about not having any clothing that another woman has worn. A lot of magazines and TV shows use the phrase "Who Wore it Best?" It's like a ploy to pit women against women and create division where there need not be any. But women, you must realize you're the most powerful force to grace this earth and you're our lifeline for the universe. There's no such thing as a dress to tell you whether or not you're validated. If you don't want to look the same, it's all in the way that you present your style.

Here's an insider trick to being a stylist: A way to make a dress someone else has work for you is to do your research on customization. The truth of the matter is there are thousands of garments made for women in the masses. If you come across a retailed dress, here's what you can do to make it your own:

- *Accessorize. It can pump up, tone down or entirely change an outfit.*
- *Get a great tailor or seamstress. They'll make the fit of your garment unique to you.*

Or you can seek out new designers entirely. Google is a great search tool. So is the Internet You can also find some of the up-and-coming, hungry and eager designers at the fashion schools (The Art Institute or Parsons). Look for a designer that caters to your features. If you a have small waist, a curvy bottom or you're flatter up top and have a difficult time finding the proper fit, this is ideal. Not only do you get the opportunity to have something that's unique, but you're also helping usher in someone's talents who may not be discovered yet. Or you can keep your designer your little secret when people always see you in something cool and interesting. You may pay a fee for customization, but there's a slim to none chance anyone will be wearing your stuff!

Examples of what to wear where:
  @ The Formal Cocktail Hour:
  - ✓ **Ultra-formal aka White Tie:** Long evening gowns
  - ✓ **Formal aka Black Tie:** Cocktail, long dresses or dressy evening separates.
  - ✓ **Semi-formal aka After Five:** Cocktail dress, little black dress, long skirt or dressy suit

- ✓ **Business Formal:** Tailored suit or professional dress; professional, not sensual
- ✓ **Cocktail Hour:** Trimmed and elegant; little black dress
- ✓ **Causal:** Sundress, relaxed blouse, polo or skirt
  NOTE: These are go-to ideas. Feel free to incorporate your personal style. Always ask if unsure!

How can a Lady maintain both class and sex appeal in fashion?
By not using her body as an ornament, but showing that it's an instrument to be proud of. When I'm shopping for a woman, I tend to look at the cuts and strong quality fabric that's going to keep its shape. I try to keep a balance. If the breasts are exposed, I try to make it so the legs are a little more toned down and covered up. The same concept applies if there's a sexy split on the side. I try to keep equilibrium between what I'm showing and what I'm not showing. The best way to be sexy is to accentuate and not exaggerate your features.

Remember, if you're going to show leg, you can be a bit more modest on top. Or if you're going to show more of your bust because that's a great feature you have, then try to be more modest toward the bottom. Know where you should draw the line. If you want to maintain class, you don't want a bunch of breasts, butt, stomach and arms hanging out. It leaves nothing to the imagination. And you know what men love? Men love the illusion of a woman's body. That's why it's so sexy when a woman wears just a T-shirt. A man has to envision her body underneath it. I've seen women wear men's shirts in photo shoots, and you don't see a whole lot of skin–just legs and a neckline. It's because you've tantalized the senses and you've made someone think.

You can be provocative, but you can also evoke a thought behind what it is that you're wearing. That is the key to being sexy. You don't have to show it, but make us think about it.

What would you suggest a woman never wears?

Ill-fitted garments. If you're going to buy something, buy something that fits. And always buy something that makes you feel incredible. There are no rules to fashion, but the common denominator of the rule to style is that you have to find something that makes you feel empowered, it has to be something that makes you feel great and it has to make you feel confident when you wear it. If it doesn't it will exude. It's definitely the fit and it's definitely the confidence. If you find a garment that evokes that within you, then you're on the right track to finding your own personal style. If you have clothes in your closet that don't make you look incredible and make you feel like the most beautiful woman in the world or the room, get rid of them. They're doing you a disservice.

Style on a Budget:

The key to finding great garments on a budget is to shop at off-price stores where you can find designer clothes at prices lower than in department or specialty stores. You might be surprised that I love going to Loehmann's, Ross and Marshalls. There are also nontraditional retailers like Target that offer pieces influenced by up-and-coming designers who people are familiar with. I also love going to places like H&M and Zara that are mid-to-low end and discovering clothing that's emulated by current designers. And don't be afraid to thrift! Go to an affluent neighborhood in your neighborhood and visit Goodwill for some awesome options!

It's the age of the Internet. You can save money by shopping around online, too. Just make sure you have a good return policy, and look for the credibility and the credentials of the stores. A Yelp search will help you find trusted reviews. Lastly, you can look for smartphone apps that that will alert you when sales are happening. It's really the age of the consumer and you have the power to get what you want at the price that you want.

These are great ideas for shopping if you don't have an ample budget.

Toye Adedipe is one of the most sought after celebrity wardrobe and fashion stylists in the business. He's worked with major television networks, films, magazines, national recording artists and media conglomerates. He's a respected designer and artist. toyeadedipe.blogspot.com

---

As you've learned, having style is about being fearless. The first time I wore a V-neck & blazer, I saw folks laughing. The second time I wore a V-neck & blazer, I saw folks wearing a V-neck & blazer. They'll laugh until everybody's doing it. Be stylish enough to do it first.

STYLE REPRESENTS YOUR DESIRE TO BE YOURSELF

Style isn't limited to clothing. Style is the way you talk. It's the way you move and the way you stand. Style is the way you handle people and handle your business. Style is how you write and how you think. You sit with your own style and dance to your own orchestra. Style provides vibrancy amidst the mundane. And when it's coupled with confidence, you win the World Series, the Super Bowl and the World Cup. Maybe not the Super Bowl and World cup, but the stylish gentlewoman finds herself in front of more bowls and cups than average–her dinner date average is above average.

What gains our attention doesn't always gain our respect. Don't confuse a cute compliment or "all eyes on you" as importance or reverence. A man will stare at a sock if it's pretty enough. Some women dress to appeal to men. Some women dress to appeal to other women. And most women dress for themselves. Do your thing, but just know that the message your clothes send might matter more than the clothes themselves. No need to make laps around lounges to be noticed – sexy is a whisper. The minute you try is the second you fail. No woman alive can do you better than yourself.

Low self-esteem ruins high fashion.

Confidence makes average attractive and a lack of it makes beauty boring. Wear what you want, but be mindful of your environment.

"You can have anything you want in life if you dress for it." - Edith Head

Lady in Red.
There's power in red. Be it red lips, a redhead, a red dress or red pumps, there's a sense of power and allure that follows the color wherever it goes.

It Looks Better in Black!

"Women who wear Black lead colourful lives."
~Neiman Marcus

You don't have to be gothic to enjoy the simplicity of black. Black speaks for you. It's your personal spokesperson that states: "I have arrived."

Black is posh. Black is elegant. Black is cool. Black is clean and gives the illusion of sleek and fit.

Be certain your blacks match. Black comes in many different shades. What you think matches can be proven otherwise under harsh light. It's best to purchase black pieces together so you're sure they match.

Bedtime.
La Perla under the sweats. Sometimes it's enough to be sexy for you and you only. Perhaps you prefer a robe or nothing at all. Just don't wear dirty daytime clothes to bed!

Trends.
Your style is what's in style. What works for you will always be best for you and look best on you because style is you internal worn externally.

Trends are suitable for the moment, but you don't have to focus on keeping up with all of them. Occasionally a trend will come around that entices you. Feel free to subscribe to the flavor of the month, but know that it will eventually lose its taste. It's always wise to invest in what's classic and what's timeless.

Arm Candy

G's on your purse isn't the same as G's in your purse – an expensive empty bag reflects its carrier.

I learned at an early age never to take candy from my mother's purse. A man has no business going in there. To this day, I'm shocked at the many things a Lady keeps in a purse. From money to mints, to makeup and meals, a woman's purse contains any option necessary for the day:

- o Healthy Snack
- o Hairbrush/Comb
- o Phone Charger
- o Sanitary Items
- o Extra pair of stockings in case yours rip.

NOTE: Using your breasts as your purse is poor public etiquette. But I'm sure perverts don't mind.

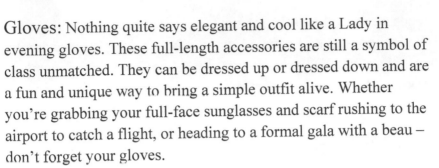

Gloves: Nothing quite says elegant and cool like a Lady in evening gloves. These full-length accessories are still a symbol of class unmatched. They can be dressed up or dressed down and are a fun and unique way to bring a simple outfit alive. Whether you're grabbing your full-face sunglasses and scarf rushing to the airport to catch a flight, or heading to a formal gala with a beau – don't forget your gloves.

Art Collecting: Darks, lights, blues, hues, clashing, passion, hands in action. The lines, the tones, the movements, the texture, the shapes–the highs, the lows, the fluids, the pressure, the mistakes–toss it up, fix your stroke–and do it again … and again … and do it again … and again, because empty walls are meant to be touched.

Art is a visual climatic culmination of thought, imagination and purpose dripped on sheets. It's the human spirit regurgitated on canvas. Art reflects culture, dictates fashion and sparks something in the mind that inspires us all to be great. It's the perfect spill.

A home without art is just a square with a roof on it–like gums with just a tooth on it, it's excess empty space. Interior design doesn't just consist of a bed, magazines and ice cream. Your home is your castle. The personality of a home is indefinable, but should reflect the charm of its owner. Your décor is a great opportunity to display style by comfortably exposing your soul. Take honor in your home. Those walls are meant to be touched, so put some art up. No, you don't have to go out and get a Munch or Basquiat. There are thousands of local talented artists to support!

I present, the art to art collecting:

- Buy it because you like it, because it moves you and because it'll enhance your life–not because you're trying to fit into some form of society.
- Once you've educated yourself and have fallen in love with a work of art, purchase it, take it home and enjoy it.
- Don't rely on others. Do your own research. Visit as many art galleries as you can. Staff can be helpful guides in art education.
- Get on gallery mailing lists so you'll be invited to openings and special events.
- Visit and join your local art museums and non-profit art centers. Curators sometimes give lectures on collecting art.
- Check to see if your city has an art walk where you can view works of art from artists in your neighborhood at your own pace. *Generally the first Friday of every month.*
- Increase your network. If you don't know any artists, Social Media stalk them. If you know art collectors, talk to them and find out what they know.
- Subscribe to some cool art magazines.
- Support independent local artists!

A big part of the pleasure in collecting art is the educational process and gradual development of greater self-confidence. Trust your instincts if you care to collect art meaningfully. Meet someone who'll take the time to educate you more in order to help with confidence in your taste. Art galleries and art shows are some of the cheapest, yet coolest dates. Learn about different artists and be prepared to add different pieces in a collection. The more you go, the more you know.

The way you begin art collecting is simple–you begin. Go slowly, ask questions and be sure you can't live without it. Build your visual vocabulary and visual literacy. This could take time, so don't rush it. There are many benefits to owning original art. The most important by far is simply for the love of it. Enjoy.

Travel: Exposure develops style. Go everywhere and see everything. Expect delays. Bring this book along on your journeys.

A Gentlewoman Writes:
Her words paint murals–her murals flow like writings. Her work is beyond the human experience. Consuming her art becomes overwhelming. It's difficult to digest such beauty in a single setting. Does such a woman exist? Writing is the art of the hand keeping pace with the mind. It's important to write things down. Not just as a means to organize the day, but to excrete your thoughts. Writing is a connection with you that keeps you in-tune with yourself. Thoughts are intended to leave the mind, but sometimes there's no one to talk to. Writing is the release. Writing is cathartic and therapeutic. It's an exercise of the mind that stimulates growth and fosters intellect. But sometimes it's best kept to yourself. Be careful when blogging or posting your thoughts online. Sometimes your frustrating and expressive words can backfire. If you can potentially lose a job, relationship or your life, limit your words to a journal…or a priest.

A Gentlewoman Reads:
A gentlewoman pursues intelligence. She's a lover of it, in fact. Reading is a great way to expand the mind. Literature allows you to learn unfamiliar words, live vicariously through others and travel the world, all without leaving your bedside. There's something to be said about a woman with a library. Book owners are beautiful. Book readers are sexy. Well, you're perusing this book, aren't you?

NOTE: You no longer have to go anywhere to get a good book. Just download your favorite author right on your smartphone, tablet or computer!

"The world is a book and those who do not travel read only one page." - St. Augustine

Beverly's Heels

Beverly's Heels: *California*

Just as shoes require their own small and separate closet, this section requires its own small and separate chapter.

I grew up in California where women dressed like women. They could be seen at the schools, supermarket or Sunday service. One particular commonality was their love for shoes. Stiletto connoisseurs gathered and discussed heels like orthopedists. A woman's affinity for shoes seemed like a love affair. I've never seen a romance so intense.

Spring heat brings out feet. If you plan on wearing open-toes, make sure your toes don't look like opened toes. A pedicure costs twenty dollars. Beware of suicide feet, a.k.a. hanging toes. They're against the law. Don't force large feet into small shoes. If it doesn't fit, you must acquit. And it's not all about your shoes. Half of us don't look down that far anyway. Forget heels, there's nothing like a woman walking in her greatness! That's what's truly sexy.

Sole searching doesn't require soul searching. After you have your basic shoes, the rest are merely a matter of choice. Don't let Cinderella and Dorothy fool you into thinking shoes can change your life. If *all* you have to show for your relationship are high heels and a handbag, you're in a fashion show, not love.

The sole of a shoe is the portion that comes in direct contact with the ground, often wearing out first. Each sole is created according to the owner of the shoes' lifestyle. A dancer uses leather outsoles to turn and glide in, while a hiker needs a thicker and more durable sole. Put your feet in someone else's shoes and you just might stumble. Don't compare yourself to others because your lifestyle is unique to your life. You're not perfect, but everyday remind yourself of how far you've come. Keep striding in greatness. But walk in the shoe soles that are meant for you.

Intermission
Throne

Throne: Art Show

No need to undress. She doesn't have to pose. She doesn't have to try. Just right there. Just like that. She's perfect.

Everyone is Beautiful.

All-Natural & PHOTOSHOP FREE – no photo editing software was used in the making of this section.

Interlude
Red Lips on a White Glass

Red Lips on a White Glass: *The Art of Wine*

-A red cab parked beside me – not a taxi, but a Sauvignon. I called for another. Traces of Ruby Woo stained the glass. I could smell the vintage on her top lip. Her skin was dark, but her lips were red. Her heels were dark, but her bottoms were red. The room was dark, but the lights were red. The perfect moment...

I demanded to have her whether in public or in private. She was sensational like that. Dripping legs, beautiful body, natural tones and a taste that made the lips jealous of the tongue with a trip to ecstasy that justified each affair. I'd grip her by the neck, as she so desired. Her arrival was my starting point. The climax was foreplay. She joined me for dinners and dialogue until becoming more involved. We were members of the Mile High Club–we flew first class together. When we'd land, she'd accompany me on yachts.

On dry land, she'd ride with me and if I got pulled over, she'd be one to get me in trouble. She was dangerous. I was addicted. She was gorgeous and distracting. I had enough. My limit had been reached, but she kept finding her way back in my hands. I called it quits and pushed her off. She filed for abuse.

Wine is a woman.
And like a woman, wine is beautifully complex. To sip great grapes stirs an emotion inside of you, no matter if you're wearing a cocktail dress at a dinner party or cloaked in a robe at home on the couch with no makeup on – a glass of red, white or blush will make any woman blush. Wine makes you feel sexy. It appeals to your five senses and conjures beautiful imagery. It serves as a conversational lubricant, while animating the shy, and turning the verbose into the contemplative. This art in a glass tastes damn good, too.

*But wine can be intimidating. There's so much to learn. Several universities are beginning to offer courses on the subject. What is it that has culture enthusiasts so enthralled? I've enlisted the help of my good friend, Jaye Price, wine educator and manager of "The Wine Shoe" in Atlanta, Georgia to find out. Grab a glass and pay attention. I humbly present to you, **The Art of Wine:***

In simple theory, wine is fermented grape juice. What makes wine an art form are the details. Over many millennia, it's been used in several religious sacraments. It's experienced development in so many ways throughout the centuries in parts of the world. What makes the art of wine cool is to see how people truly appreciate it just like any other form of art: performance art, musical art or visual art. Wine is a reflection of a particular community, culture, region and style. It's reflective of the climate, the lifestyle and the cuisines. When you go to a wine tasting, you're traveling the world.

There are thousands of grapes, but many people are familiar with only about eight grape varietals. We're not necessarily a wine culture. America, in general, is a very young country – whereas other wines have been around for thousands of years. Read the pages of Gilgamesh, and you'll find descriptions of wine. In the Bible through Genesis you'll see wine referenced. But in America, we still have a slight taboo from a cultural and religious standpoint.

The coolness of wine is that you can taste grape varietals from a Bordeaux blend coming from France and taste that same exact blend coming from California, but the experience will be completely different. It's a matter of old world versus new world wines. Old world wines are primarily from old world countries in Europe and very much reflective of the climate, terrain and region which it's from. New world wines are the product of colonization. People came over to North and South America, South Africa and Australia and they brought grape varietals from Europe. Many of the wines we enjoy domestically– Cabernet, Chardonnay, Pinot Grigio–aren't indigenous grapes to our land. They were brought over by missionaries, monks and priests. These grapes have been cultivated over the years with a method similar to Europe's. The difference is our climate and lifestyle and the wine is reflective of that. North America has indigenous grapes commonly referred to as Native American grapes (Muscadine and Sustanon).

To say I'm drinking a wine from a particular region like a *Bordeaux*, a *Barolo* or *Chianti* is like saying I'm drinking an *Atlanta*, a *Riverdale* or a *Buckhead*. It describes the area from which it comes from. If I'm having wine from California, it's so much more about the grape than it is about the area and land in which it comes from. These are some of the distinctive characteristics that make wine so appealing. The tannins, the acidity, the sugar and alcohol contents; whether it grew in warmer or cooler climates, or how far it grew from the ocean. If I'm listening to a Mozart sonata or concerto, I can differentiate between Mozart versus Saleiri. These are two different composers from the same era, but there are certain elements that make Mozart who he is and Saleiri who he is. The same goes for wine.

This is what the art and mere appreciation is about. As sophisticates and cultured people, you go to galleries, ballets, operas and museums to enjoy the finer things in life. You enjoy great food, fashion and clothing. Clothing is only intended to blanket your body and keep you warm, but fashion is the art of clothing. You're paying attention to the details or the exact functionality of a particular ensemble. You might dress to capture the look of a certain time period or dress to go to *this* event versus *that* event. A drink is supposed to keep your thirst quenched, but wine is the art of consumption. You might drink a particular wine for *this* meal versus *that* meal. Many times, we don't think of wine in an artistic fashion because we're very much into the inebriation aspect of it. That's just an added benefit. From the temperature at which the wine is served, to the glassware, it's all art. The reality is you can just pop a cork and drink from the bottle, but to truly enjoy a wine and the process it went through, you must respect the art.

To being to explore further, understand what it is that you like from a wine. Are you smitten by the fruit characteristic; do you like the minerality or earthiness; do you like the light and the crispness or boldness of a wine? Really find out what style of wine you enjoy. The more you read and the more you taste, the better you'll be able to appreciate the subtle complexities of a wine. Always drink what you like. Don't let anyone tell you what to drink or what not to drink. It's also important to articulate why you like something and why you don't like something. You may never come in contact with the same house or particular varietal again, but if you can articulate the characteristics you enjoy, you can always get what you're looking for in another bottle.

Once you've found the wine that you enjoy, take a seat and allow a sommelier to serve you. Your server will present a wine list to you. Don't be afraid to ask questions. That's why they're there. Once ordered, the sommelier will come by to show you the unopened wine's label so you can verify that the wine that's arrived is indeed the wine you ordered. The sommelier will wait for you to check the label for the varietal, vintage and producer. If everything checks out, the bottle will be opened and the cork presented to you. Check for mold or cracks in the wood. Once the test is passed, your wine will be served in a small amount for its first inspection. This is what's called the *Five S's of Wine Tasting*. **Sight** | **Swirl** | **Smell** | **Sip** | **Savor**.

1. The **sight** is to check for visual flaws. A cloudiness or film is a sign of the wine going bad. You don't want cork residue in the wine either. Sight can also determine the age of the wine by its color components – aged reds tend to get lighter, while aged whites tend to get darker.
2. **The swirl** is about the breathing of the wine. It helps open the wine up. This goes on throughout the process of you enjoying the beautiful beverage. Hold the glass by its stem.

3. **The smell** is about picking up the bouquet, which is used for mature wines. The aroma is often associated with younger wines.

4. **The sip** is about tasting the different characteristics on the tongue, cheek and the top of the mouth. You'll pick up the acidity; how round it is; how much fruit is on the pallet; how tannic it might be; whether it has oak or has been fermented in stainless steel. A decanter can be used for bolder reds that are higher in tannins. As a natural preservative, tannins come from the skin of the grapes and give bold wines its dry sensation. Decanters help wine to breathe in order to soften tannins and decrease the bold taste. Never judge a wine on the first taste. Once the cork has been opened and the gasses have been released, the wine is going to continually change in both the glass and bottle because it's stopped fermenting. Your brain might not process the shock. Maybe the flavor of your chewing gum, toothpaste or food initially got in the way. The second and third tastes matter more. If you taste vinegar, it's a sign of the wine going bad. Have your sommelier grab another bottle.

5. **To savor** is the final step. All good things must come to an end, but this is just the beginning. If the wine is in good standing, give your sommelier the approval, and your guests will be served. Cheers to an attractive evening with elegant company.

Jaye Price | Wine Educator | Jazz Musician | Wineshoeatlanta.com

Wine is a woman. Take your time with her. Over time you'll begin to understand, furthermore enjoy this gorgeous experience. You might want to create a wine journal (Crate & Barrel - Beverly Hills or mobile app). Carry it in your clutch, documenting and analyzing each wine in the journal. Describe your emotions and write your own reviews instead of relying on others. Either way, a wine journal will be a useful and enjoyable reference in years to come.

Old etiquette states: a Lady never gets drunk | New etiquette states: Wine is the classiest way to do it.

Enjoy responsibly | ⊘ *drinking & driving | Twenty-one +*

Cabernet – Associated with cherry, olive or plum
Chardonnay – Paired with apple, lemon or melon
Pinot Noir – Similar to zinfandel with earthiness, peppercorn and lavender
Riesling – Compared to grapefruit, jasmine and cinnamon
Zinfandel – Generally associated with blackberry, pomegranate and wood

Favorable Wine Serving Temperatures:
White Wines: 54-58 °F or 12-14 °C
Red Wines: 58-64 °F or 14-18 °C
Rosé Wines: 45-55 °F or 7-13 °C
Sparkling Wines: 42-52 °F or 6-11 °C
Fortified Wines: 55-68 °F or 13-20 °C

Art of the Toast

Chinese: *Wen lie!*
Dutch: *Proost!*
English: *Cheers!*
Finnish: *Kippis!*
French: *A votre sante!*
German: *Prosit!*
Greek: *Yasas!*
Hawaiian: *Okole maluna!*
Hebrew: *L'Chayim!*
Irish: *Slainte!*
Italian: *Alla salute!*
Japanese: *Kampai!*
Kippis! *Brazilian: Saoede!*
Polish: *Na Zdrowie!*
Russian: *Na zdorovia!*
Spanish: *Salud!*
Swedish: *Skal!*

"May you live all the days of your life!"

Tender

Tender: *Emotions*

"For the love of money is the root of all evil, which while some coveted after, they have erred from the faith, and pierced themselves through with many sorrows."
-1 Timothy 6:10

The quote above is often misquoted. There's nothing wrong with the frequent acquisition of money. It's necessary to have tender if you intend on being a citizen. However, it's the **love** of money that gets people in all sorts of trouble. Money should never be your god.

The love of tender brings about tender emotions. People don't talk about money. They don't like to. Asking a Lady how much she makes is like asking an overweight virgin if she's having a boy or a girl—it's rude. Between politics and religion, money-talk is considered taboo in most forms of society. It's the reason people lie, cheat, steal and kill. There's so much emotion tied to decimals and dollars that folks will lay down their lives for it.

If your house is in order, your family is in order and your career is in order, there's absolutely no reason why your money shouldn't be in order. But money-talk can be intimidating. It's like God saved all the biggest and most confusing words for finance. Don't fret – comprehensive financial literacy isn't reserved for the privileged.

This chapter focuses on financial etiquette:

Seek trusted professional financial advice prior to making any money decisions.

Saving: Let's get this out of the way – saving money must become a priority. It's not just about storing it away somewhere and never seeing it again. Saving will help secure your future. It serves as an emergency fund so you don't rely on credit cards. That means you can stop borrowing other people's money for what you need and spending your money on what you want! Saving allows you to know what you spend and spend what you've got, so you're not going into debt. Most importantly, saving allows you to build wealth. It's a commitment to you, your family and your community at large.

PEOPLE DON'T LIKE DISCIPLINE – THEY JUST LIKE THE RESULTS

Always pay yourself first, but save more than you spend. It's not all that bad to be cheap. But let's call it frugality; that just sounds better. Carry cash when you can. People psychologically have more of a connection to cash than cards. Cash is much more difficult to let go compared to pulling out a plastic card and swiping it. Cash is king when it comes to getting the greatest deals! Always negotiate when appropriate. This doesn't mean try to get a deal on a pack of gum at a convenient store's cash register. But use your bargaining power frequently and courteously. The dumbest question is the question that goes unasked. Sometimes all it takes is an inquiry with smile. Lastly, learn to delay instant gratification and don't be embarrassed by coupons. You'll have to adjust to some lifestyle changes and break some spending habits. And don't expect anyone else to step in for those areas you've decided to be frugal in. You can still go out and have a good time, but if you arrived broke, got in free and call a man cheap for not sponsoring your drink at the bar...you're a panhandler.

NOTE: *Be careful when maneuvering about the day with cash. Put it somewhere safe and always be attentive when and where you pull it out. We live in a dangerous world!*

Plan: If you woke up with one million dollars in your account, what would you do with it? Everyone wants more money, but what's your reason? You must have a plan for your *grands*. It's similar to having a teenage kid. You must tell it what to do, where to go and know when it's going to come back.

"...THE BORROWER IS SLAVE TO THE LENDER." –PROVERBS 22:7

If you're in debt, get out. Draw up a monthly non-negotiable budget and follow it religiously. Don't worry; basic clothing can be included in the budget. You don't have to feel guilty about shopping when you assign and control your money.

BUDGET BASICS:
- o Food
- o Home/Shelter/Utilities
- o Transportation
- o Basic Clothing

Anything else is extra and you can budget according to your plan.

Investing: The work doesn't stop once the debt is gone, the savings account is full of 3-6 months of expenses and the money is rolling in. But you can finally begin to work smarter, not harder. You do so by investing! Conserving money overtime in the right environment(s) creates wealth. Seek trusted professional financial advice and make your money make money for you. Money market accounts from mutual fund companies are a good start.

Giving: You didn't think this was all about you, did you? There's no greater gift than the sacrifice of self. Pour back into those in need. Don't give blindly, but do give. Don't allow the deception and greed of others to taint the beauty of giving. Don't let thieves rob you of your heart to give. Give and it will be given back to you. No matter how much money you have, you're still going to die, so why solely focus on storing up what will perish? You can run out of money, but you can't run out of love. You can't run out of serving others. Real money is measured in what you do with it, not how much you have. So don't save to spend just for self, but save to be selfless. If you want it, be willing to work a lot making a little so you can work a little making a lot. Success requires sacrifice. Be prepared for a marathon–what's worth having isn't easy to acquire.

Money alone doesn't make you successful. Success is whatever you say it is. When you set goals and meet them, you're successful. But some people require your bank statement to measure your triumph. When they can show you their lives are balanced, you can show them your account balance. Your money is no one's business but your own. If you're married, then it becomes the business of your spouse. Money can become an issue in your relationship if you let it. Financial related fights are the number one cause of divorce in North America. Many men tragically have our self-worth and purpose tied to money because it's how we're taught to provide. If the money isn't right, we might not be right. That's a shame and I hope the men reading this realize it's wise to rely on the real supplier of our needs, not the tool that directs the transaction. You can run out of money, but you can't run out of

God–prayer does what money can't. Put your priorities in focus. If you *chase* money and I *chase* God, let's see who *wins*...

Such a Lady

Such a Lady: *Contemporary Gentlewomen*

It's difficult to trust people who can't keep friends. Among many qualities, being a gentlewoman is about sisterhood.

You don't have to hate men to be about sisterhood, but man can't fulfill the role that women play in each other's lives. The best friendships are organic, and sisterhood is the healthy ingredient to any contemporary gentlewoman. Your sisterhood is your safe place. It's sacred. You laugh together, cry and build. You heal, you grow and you release. This association is designed by love and built on trust. There exists no envy or judgment. You are the sum of your sisters. You represent them and they represent you.

The collective is always more important than the individual

Oh, what a beautiful collective. There's Ms. Ambitious who doesn't know what fear looks like. She's accomplished much, but always has her eyes set on more! She isn't boastful and doesn't pretend to know it all, but she motivates those around her through her actions.

Then there's Ms. Plain Jane. The world wouldn't be balanced without her. She's consistent, but not predictable. She's not into fashion or makeup because she's a different person with different interests. But she's still a gentlewoman because she *holds down* whatever she's doing. Jane has her own walk, her own individuality and own style. There's only one of her and she lives up to it! She is important. She matters. The world needs her.

Ms. Organic is a treat! You can always catch her at a low-key eatery with an organic meal and some blush wine. She's into yoga and art. She's the friend who's passionate about people, but never afraid to get her hands dirty. She doesn't mistake movement for progress.

Introducing: Ms. Single and Sexy...and Satisfied. She's strong and she's sassy. Her walkaway could win wars. She understands that marriage doesn't validate her as a woman, her own gender does. This Lady is too busy being great in a great city with her own great hobbies and dynamic personality. She's paved her own beautiful lane and fully understands that happiness is an inside job. Her humility radiates and intellect shines through. She embraces exactly who she is and has fun with it. She doesn't seem to take life too seriously, but is serious about life. It's OK to be both beautiful and timid, and at times insecure–she's all three. She's human. She's a gentlewoman.

Then there's Ms. Just Like You. Sometimes her insecurities get the best of her. Being *gorgeous at all times* is too much pressure. Those small dresses and awkward heels are difficult to walk in. She'd rather watch TV on the couch with ice cream and pass gas. She's sarcastic and honest and might even have motivational conversations with herself. She dislikes certain aspects of her body and her life, but she's working to improve on them. Accept her for who she is because she's many of women. She's beautiful. She's a gentlewoman.

There's Ms. Late Bloomer who might not have started living life until her 40s. Maybe she put her family before herself and her career. The kids are grown now and she finally realized that you only live life once! Catch Ms. Bloomer out and about with the best of them. She gives younger women a run for their money. If this is you, pour yourself a glass of wine tonight. You deserve it!

Hello Superwoman! Perhaps you've accomplished it all. You're a powerful gentlewoman about town who's mastered her education, her social circle and her goals. How do you find balance? I spoke with Congresswoman Barbara Lee who had this to say:

"How you define your personhood is up to you. I don't think it's hard to find a balance. I went to school because I wanted to be something. I wanted to learn. I wanted to work and get a job and take care of my kids. Finding the balance wasn't an issue for me because I know I'm a woman. It's not like I had to struggle with it. It's up to a woman to determine what her femininity should be. Not every woman thinks having kids is part of being feminine and certainly there are plenty women who don't have kids who are feminine."

I agree. It's you who makes you a woman. Not a man or a family. Without those things, you're still a Lady.

Many men socialize by insulting each other and not meaning it, while many women socialize by complimenting each other and not meaning it

Women aren't natural enemies. You've been taught to believe that. Don't worry about her. Instead, be a resource to her. Mentor her. That's where the power is. Her success isn't your failure. Her pretty doesn't take away from your beauty. That insecurity will lead to envy, and envy makes you hate someone you don't even know. Confident women have no issue embracing other beautiful women. Just because she possesses something you don't doesn't make you any less of a woman. God created you specifically. Enjoy you! Being jealous is just a terrible excuse for complacency. It's an easy way to justify unmerited hatred. Never envy what you haven't earned. It's tragic to hate other's success when you haven't experienced other's sacrifices. Envy is reserved for the lazy, uninspired and unwilling, so you can't be upset by the results you didn't get with the work you didn't do. To resent someone's blessing takes away from your own. There's nothing more beautiful than discovering your own destiny and spilling yourself onto it.

Hater | ˈhātər | noun: Someone who can't understand why their fantasies are your realities.

A beautiful lady who gossips forfeits her beauty. Keep in mind that those who gossip with you will gossip about you. Be wise. Be warned. Gentlewomen don't discuss people they don't like. Their names don't even come up. If you're constantly talking badly about someone, you likely want something she/he has. Maybe you can't figure out how they got it or don't think they deserve it. Figure out what that's about and fix it. Taking on that kind of personal responsibility is healing.

"GREAT MINDS DISCUSS IDEAS; AVERAGE MINDS DISCUSS EVENTS; SMALL MINDS DISCUSS PEOPLE."
–ELEANOR ROOSEVELT

Sip wine and relax! No one is out to get you. Your only competition is in the mirror. What God has for you is for you. Celebrate your existence. That *catty* stuff is for the *birds*!

Evaluate your space

Be careful – enemies are courteous, too. Not everyone is meant for your life. I encourage you to study your circle. Some stepsisters have got to go. Spring-cleaning includes people. But some people are people hoarders – they need their own special on A&E. They can never have enough associates, friends, best friends, besties or BFFs.

Stop picking women apart; stop tearing women down. Tell a sister good morning. Ask a stranger how she's doing. Be intentional about reaching out. Love disarms people and you never know what another might be going through.

If you want to be successful, keep honest people around. God is the ultimate decider of your destiny, but He uses honest people to help. All hail to sisterhood!

Caution:
Be wise. Not every toast is made with honorable intent. Be careful. The same hand used to shake can be used to stab. But your sisters operate on a higher standard. Your bond is never compromised or broken. Arguments are fleeting. Bruises heal. Hurt feelings are repairable. And men are replaceable. Let nothing or let no one stand in the way of your brilliant sisterhood. You need them and they need you.

Adjust your crown.

Royal Courting

Royal Courting: *The Etiquette of Dating*

Is this what you came for?

Extra! Extra! Read All About It!

Singlehood is the new STD – nobody wants it, but one in every five Americans has it. Biological clocks are ticking off women into terrible relationships. The fear has generated a nationwide epidemic of unhealthy eagerness among countless women and the symptoms seem to be spreading. This fascination with finding Mr. Right has caused a role reversal so severely that *thirsty* women are dehydrated from chasing after men. Their vision is blurred and their desperate search is causing dizziness and confusion. Some Ladies are even sleeping with tears and broken hearts just so they're sleeping with something. But sleeping with the pain won't cure the pain. To treat an illness, one needs the proper medication – and to deal with singleness, one needs the proper partner. But there's a secret I must let you in on–single isn't a sickness, it's usually the cure!

The concept of being alone is a beautiful one. Alone is where you face flaws and accept insecurities. It's a time where you're forced to deal with the one person you like to avoid most–yourself. If you refuse to deal with you, be damn certain we will too.

Making the decision to live your life for yourself can be a rewarding feeling. Of course it's important to have an awareness of others and be kind, but don't allow negative outside opinions to affect how you live your life. Whether it's constant pressure from your mother, music or movies, the message society sends that a woman's worth is in her marital status is a lousy lie. Society suggests that if a Lady is single and successful, then she isn't successful. This piece of fiction births insecurity and breeds desperation. It's OK to want something badly and channel the desire to ambition, but never desperation. Your insecurities are like a drop of blood in a sea of sharks. Live your worth or be eaten alive. Don't let alone get you in trouble. Don't let sympathy make you compromise beliefs.

Perhaps the roses left on a co-workers desk serve as a painful reminder you sleep alone at night. But you don't know what it took for her to get those flowers. They were sent to her because her man beat her the night before. But all you see are flowers. You don't know a stranger's story. Stop comparing your life to lies. That green grass you envy might very well be artificial turf.

Don't worry about the dates other women go on. Stop comparing your training to her highlight reel. Maybe she's mastered the art of loving herself. We're attracted to that. Don't question your worth because you don't get the same kind of attention another woman gets. Some men only go after what's easily attainable. Perhaps you wouldn't want that kind of attention if you knew what it came with. Don't grow weary in doing well. Be unmoved in your high heels, head held high and high standards. A relationship won't help you if you haven't helped yourself.

Ignore your mother's rants about finding a husband. Inform her that a man who finds a wife finds a good thing. You weren't put on this earth to give your mom grandbabies. You're too busy loving yourself, so if a man desires your time, he'll have to love you more. It's foolish to discount a woman's accomplishments because she's unmarried. Marriage is a choice, not an obligation.
The reality is a happily single person is just as happy as a happily

married person. Focus on happy, not status. You're too excellent to
be worried about spending your life alone. Several men aren't
thinking about marriage, but there are several who are. That's no
concern of yours. Your concern should be you. I can't stress
enough that we pay attention to you when you pay attention to you.
A woman's greatest assets and attributes are revealed when she's
on her own journey of self-discovery. At your very best, you will
attract the exact person intended for you. No gimmicks required

Society is sending the wrong message and everyone is listening,
but not enough women are listening to themselves. Your soul lets
you know when your mind and body are prepared to properly love.
Having a man is just the icing on life's cake. You were born with
what you need. The sun doesn't look to electrical outlets for power.
Stop searching in relationships for the thing you should be
supplying for yourself. We all have the desire to be loved, but an
unhealthy eagerness for it can leave a Lady single, desperate and
lonely and a gentleman lost, oversexed and insecure. These two
likely wouldn't make a good couple. Unfortunately this describes
many partners today. When a woman is truly secure and ready for
love, a good man will take notice.

Personal Opinion Only: The sexiest position a woman can be in
is on her knees praying, so before you claim you need *a man*, you
better get used to saying *Amen*. A focus on getting a guy before a
focus on getting God is backward, and you'll probably end up with
a god spelled backward. Focus on who you're meant to be, not
who you're meant to be with.

Don't believe the hype! Being single is never as bad as society
makes it out to be. It's a choice. Some Ladies are too busy doing

the *Single Ladies* dance to care to notice Mr. Right is right in front of them.

Other women are too busy planning their wedding before planning their marriage or even being a marriage candidate. They're always bridesmaids, but never brides. I tell them if you plan your wedding prior to planning your marriage then you'll probably prepare to plan your divorce.

But then there's you. You're the strong woman with a great career, financial independence and sex appeal on a whole other level because you realize that your worth isn't determined by what a man chooses to do. You have your life together and desire a man that has the same. It doesn't make you stuck up – it makes you smart. There are good and ready men who are just as ready for love as you are. You just haven't had the opportunity to meet yet. So in your time of self-love and development, don't be afraid of alone. Until you're ready and a true gentleman who exceeds your standards comes along, celebrate your single like a singer with a hit song on the Billboard Hot 100 chart. Don't sell yourself short for warm champagne, cheap cologne and a smile. There's absolutely nothing wrong with being single. Please enjoy yourself.

The Lady hardest to get is the easiest to keep.

Being hard to get is more about discernment and less about playing games. Requiring a man to work hard for something generally makes him appreciate it that much more. A great Lady challenges a good man to be an even better man. The Lady who made me wait two years to taste her lips is the Lady I proudly call my wife.

Some of you are ready for more. You've made personal growth, social development, education and your career your primary focuses. But you've also created a space for dating. You're prepared to meet someone who tickles your fancy. You might be open to the idea of love. Or maybe you're just ready to break the monotony and shake things up a bit. Whatever the case, there are nights you don't want to dine alone. You want to go dancing in a sexy new dress and have a drink with someone you trust. Maybe it'll be the start of something serious, maybe not.

You rush into the scene only to have your bubble busted instantaneously. Dating comes with guidelines. Most people skim over the instructions like an online *User Agreement*. They scroll right through and click *Agree* without reading the fine print. Like any other relationship, dating requires etiquette. This chapter is the fine print. Don't skip over it. Take all that applies and ignore what doesn't. Let's get into it.

The Thought: You want to date. Sounds fun, right? Well it should be. But you must understand what dating is. Dating isn't a relationship title. Dating is an elimination process that eventually leads to who you're going to be with. It should be approached that way. New dates should be casual. You're just getting to know someone. Don't put all your eggs in one basket. Navigating relations is a bit trickier today. As men, we have all these questions that go through our head: "Who asks?" "If I ask, will she think I'm too forward?" "Who pays for the date?" "Do we split the bill?" All of these uncertainties sometimes cause us to avoid dating altogether. We'll opt for just *hanging out* with you instead.

The Scene: High heels and Heinekens decorate the room like art. It feels like summer and that's exactly what you look like. Your senses are excessively satisfied though you haven't ingested any drug–you've only entered through the door. Rehab is discouraged. Champagne is the appetizer. Music for dinner, he looks like dessert – and you might need an Advil for breakfast. The scene is set with bachelors with bachelor's...some have their master's and there are even gentlemen with PhD's. Good people celebrating great times. You might get approached; you might not.

Dating is a buyer's market for any decent guy with game. We've gotten lazy and you've gone right along with it. Even you good women have lowered your standards to the point that we don't have to pursue you. We don't have to call – you'll accept our text messages. We don't have to take you out and build a relationship – we have far too many options to waste our time and money on that. You're willing to accept a half-assed version of us to ensure your bed isn't empty at night. But if you offer better, you deserve better, so do better. A piece of a man is like a piece of a one hundred dollar bill–worthless. If he's not offering his all, peace him out. Anyone available physically, but not emotionally is unavailable.

If you're just looking to have a good time and don't wish for anything serious, then communicate that. Not every woman desires commitment and you're entitled to exactly what you want. Just be honest and upfront about your intentions. Just as you don't want a misleading man leading you on, don't lead us on.

It could be fun, you might meet someone cool, but sometimes the scene is just too damn messy. It gets tiring after a while. It becomes difficult to maneuver through the BS and filter out the garbage. Try something new! Go somewhere different and you'll meet someone different. Or focus on what's already there. Make a list of your closest male friends. Now cross out all family members and unavailable men and notice who's left. He's your good friend and confidant. He's always there when you need him. He genuinely looks forward to seeing you and even gives you fair dating advice. He might be the man who loves you and has for years. Don't discredit him because he's your homie. The greatest relationships start with the greatest friendships. Sometimes the friend zone is exactly where a man needs to be.

The Approach: *Chanel N°5* and *Tobacco Vanille* linger on white sheets. A suspicion of the private blend assures you he's present again this evening. You remember the first time. Friends greet you as you enter. You hover an index finger in the air motioning them to wait just a second. In just that second, you spot him for the second time. It's better than the first. For a second, you think you're in love. Maybe it's the wine. He approaches and compliments your familiar fragrance. You tell him it's mixed – he tells you he's mixed a few drinks. It's crowded. This conversation is meant for four ears. His hand sends electricity through your entire human experience as he leads you to VIP. He walks like a ball player. Waitresses carry complimentary cheesecake flavored chocolate covered strawberries and delicious drinks in trays for your convenience. He reaches his hand down. It's wet! Just some spilled champagne. He steps closer as he delivers a two-step. You take two steps in closer. His skin manages to fall on your lips. "You smell good," he whispers, "but taste better." Captivating. He's charming. You're alluring. He's attracted to you and attractive to you. You find him to be bereolaesque. It happened so fast. You don't have work in the morning because it's Labor Day, but this Labor Day party might be the reason you go into labor. Beverages pour. Your vision becomes blurry. Memory fades. Sunbeams piercing through blinds wake you. Your yawn is slow. *Chanel* and *Tobacco Vanille* as you inhale. A familiar fragrance lost in your pillow. Your bed is empty, but all five senses satisfied.

OK, so maybe it doesn't happen like that for you.

Maybe he whistled at you. Perhaps he had you at *hello*. Well if he whistled, tell him catcalls are reserved for the lower animal kingdom…and they make you walk faster. You're a gentlewoman. How you're approached plays a factor in whether or not you're interested. Sometimes a bad approach can destroy our chances even if you find us attractive. Yet and still, a man afraid to approach before the relationship might be afraid to take initiative during the relationship. He might be the type to respond to all of your inquiries with, "Whatever you want to do, or wherever you'd like to go, dear) Take note.

Not every woman is bitter – Sometimes he's just wack and you're not interested.

And that's OK! A whistle and a compliment don't mean a thing. You have the right to not be interested. You owe no one an explanation or answer. But do have tact in your rejection. There isn't a need for an attitude or to be mean or rude. Consider some consideration when letting a man down because we deal with rejection daily. We don't want sympathy. I just want you to understand that it's best to treat people better than they treat you— yes even those guys.

Never tolerate harassment, but walk for a moment in our shoes. It takes courage to approach and address an anonymous beautiful woman. We don't know how you'll react or if you'll think we're crazy. All of this is going through our minds with each step closer in your direction. Rejection tastes terrible. It's bitter. Even a confident man can have reservations at times. You women are genius at acting like you don't notice when an attractive man walks in a room. You notice. A Lady can pay a man no mind, hardly speak and walk on by, but want him badly. Sometimes we wouldn't mind a hint.

INTEREST vs. CHASING

The only man acceptable of being chased after is God or the guy who stole your purse. Actually, I wouldn't recommend that. So how does a Lady *approach* a man? Great question. The traditional gentleman in me says, "A man always approaches a Lady." But the contemporary gentleman in me realizes this places your fate in the hands of man, which is a ridiculous notion. There are new rules. Dating is fair game. Let's cancel all subscriptions to contradictions. There are several things a Lady can do to a capture a man's attention without appearing *desperate* or aggressive.

Not every man will boldly approach the attractive woman with her arms folded and the look of "please leave me the hell alone" on her face. It's traditionally true that men are expected to approach women, but women shouldn't abuse this fact by making the encounter unpleasant. Decline kindly and get on with it. If a man is rude or persistent and you feel like your safety is threatened, go ahead and give him your number–but not your personal number. Just like it's wise to have an extra email account to filter junk mail through, it's wise to have an extra phone number to filter junk men through. Set up a free Google Voice account and you'll be assigned a phone number. Most people use it for business, but you can use it to give to persistent and irritating men all in your business that need to mind their business.

The reality is women have been *approaching* men since the beginning of time. What I mean when I say *approaching* is that a woman orchestrates the pace, flow and direction of potential romantic encounters. A Lady can gauge the emotional climate of a room the second she walks into it. The feminine aura of a gentlewoman sets the tone of the attention she'll capture and who will be lured into her zone. A Lady knows what she's doing. The way to *approach* a man includes, but isn't limited to the following:

- o Body language: When you enjoy life, your body reflects that. When you see something you like, your body reflects that as well. Don't be afraid to allow your body to naturally express itself. Smile if he's cute and play with your hair if he's sexy. We're watching!

- o Pay Attention: Sometimes it's the man who's vying for your attention. Our signals are different than yours, but we have them. We may boldly hold an extended glance or detach ourselves from a group of friends in order to be noticed. Pay attention to our attention. Show us you're watching. Glance twenty-two seconds too long. A little longer.

- o Mild Flirting: Whisk by more than once. Make your presence known in a subtle, yet feminine way and then move on. An interested suitor will take notice and come to you. You won't have to lift a finger. We seek you harder when we know that you're focused on more than just us. You can follow up with a detailed compliment (that tie goes great with your smile), or by asking for the time when you obviously have a watch on. Don't depend solely on signals.

If interested in a man, gracefully put yourself in a position to be seen. It's only as complicated as you make it. A tiny bit of research in the person you're interested in won't hurt. Next time you see him by your car, ask if he has jumper cables (who cares if your car works perfectly fine). You can at least get a name.

A Lady *pursues* a man she's interested in by accepting his advances or by flirting. She *values* him by loving him. A man who needs more than this may want to look for it in the mirror. It's only hard to find a good man because you don't have to look, we'll find you. If none of this is for you, it's OK to make the first move and approach. If interested, we'll take the lead from there.

NOTE: An interested man is usually eager to secure your time. If he's not making plans, he doesn't want to be your man. It's both tragic and unnecessary to chase men around. Show an interested gentleman slight interest and watch us move mountains. Make no mistake; you don't want anyone who doesn't desire you enough to pursue you.

The Date: This is the part most people get wrong. But why? Dating is supposed to be fun. Know what type of dater you are.

THE SERIOUS DATER: You're not interested in dating just to date. You'd like to date with a purpose, a goal and a plan. You know exactly what it is that you want and you don't have time to play around. You'll scare a lot of men off, but that's the point. Your elimination process might be fast-paced and can grow overwhelming. Just like fishing, patience and faith are required. Also like fishing, you have to go where you'll find a good catch. Go where your ideal beau would go. If you're interested in a bookworm, go to contemporary libraries and bookstores. If you're attracted to intelligent artistic gentlemen, frequent galleries and local art walks. Be proactive and don't be so serious that you become a nuisance. Just know there's a man out there actively on the same search you're on.

THE CASUAL DATER: Nothing you observe is wrong. He's a nice guy and attractive, but he's not mesmerizing or memorable. Serious dating can be frustrating. Perhaps you need to shift your focus. Casual dating might be for you. Have some fun! Casual dating comes with no contracts. These engagements aren't marriage engagements and the dinners aren't rehearsal dinners. When you view dating casually as opposed to looking at it like an engagement or something that can lead to an engagement, you'll probably enjoy it more and you'll find the proper person –or people– to enjoy it with. Besides, you'll have more horrible first date stories to look back on and laugh at. If you change your approach to dating, you'll experience dating in a totally different way.

On the contrary, you're human and sometimes feelings get involved even when you don't plan for them to. When you date casually, you can become jaded maneuvering your way through dinners and dial tones. Casual dating is involuntary manslaughter. You have no intention of bringing death to emotions, killing feelings or breaking hearts, but it's bound to happen to all parties involved. Do think you can handle this? Proceed with caution.

First Official Date: In these untruthful times, *Google* should be your first date. It's best to play it safe. If he's picking you up, text your friends his phone number so they have it. If you prefer to be extra cautious, memorize his license plate on the way to the car door and jot it down in your phone. This should be the last time you pick up your mobile device. Have some decency and try to enjoy yourself.

Did he arrive with flowers? Well, maybe he's trying to tell you something.

Decoding Flowers:

Do you know that plants and flowers have specific meanings? Single stems could serve as sweet love letters; while pedals write paragraphs and bouquets become sonnets. The next time you receive an exotic bloom, you'll know exactly what the sender is trying to say:

Camellia: Perfection.

Carnation (general): Fascination; distinction.

Cattail: Peace and prosperity.

Chrysanthemum: For a wonderful friend.

Chrysanthemum (red): Good luck and best wishes.

Chrysanthemum (white): Truth.

Daffodil: You're the only one. ⬅️ Perhaps it's too soon for this!

Daisy: Innocence; purity; gentleness.

Gardenia: For your secret (not-so-secret anymore) love.

Heather: Admiration and solitude.

Hyacinth (purple): I'm sorry; please forgive me.

Hyacinth (pink): Playful nature.

Hyacinth (white): Loveliness; I'll pray for you.

Hydrangea: Thank you for understanding.

Iris: Faith and hope; wisdom and valor; my compliments.

Larkspur: Lightness and swiftness.

Lily (general): Purity of the heart.

Lily (calla): Beauty.

Lily (tiger): Wealth.

Lily (white): Innocence, purity, sweetness and majesty.

Lily (yellow): Gratitude.

Lily of the Valley: Return to happiness; humility.

Magnolia: Nobility.

Mistletoe: Kiss me; affection; to surmount difficulties.

Orchid: Beauty, refinement and wisdom.

Orchid: Mature charm.

Petunia: Your presence soothes me.

Snapdragon: Gracious; protection from evil.

Stock: Bonds of affection; promptness.

Sunflower: Power; warmth; nourishment.

Tulip (general): Gift from a perfect lover.

Violet: Faithfulness; modesty.

We Dined: Relax. You deserve an evening with a gent. Shall we? But if you only accepted the date for the free meal, then go to a homeless shelter. Better yet, go down the aisles of *Costco* for the free samples. If you always have your hand out with nothing to contribute, then we're on a date with a panhandler. It's not only inconsiderate, but impolite go out with someone for ulterior motives. But you knew that already.

Now back to the date. If you're meeting him at the restaurant, this is one of the rare times where arriving a few minutes late is acceptable. After all, you wear the crown. Allow him to revel in the suspense, but ensure your arrival is better than the anticipation. Don't keep him waiting too long. If you'll be more than ten minutes late, what was once cute just became disrespectful. Place a courtesy text or call to update the patient gentleman about the details. An apology would be pleasant, as well.

If you're arriving together, allow the beau to be a gentleman and open your car door. Perhaps he took notice that your clothes are complicated and your heels are unforgiving, so he was considerate and valet parked. In this case, the concierge will open your door as your date settles the attendant's gratuity. Now let's go inside.

The reservations have been made and hopefully the wait is brief. This is where you can engage in small talk, but nothing too heavy. Save the bold dialogue until after the bold wine has been poured. He might compliment you and you might smile. A great way to let us know you're interested is to compliment us first. It heightens our level of confidence in the moment and helps set the tone for the rest of the evening. The hostess calls out Mr. & Mrs. (his last). Don't be startled. He was just trying to be adorable. Maybe it's too soon. Now let's have a seat.

No need to reach, he'll pull out your chair. If it's finer dining, a server will do it for you. Remove the napkin/serviette from in front of you and place it in your lap. But you knew that already because gentlewomen know how to properly dine. In case you forgot… Here's a quick reference.

Table Etiquette:
Elbows on the table are OK when in conversation or when waiting for the food. However, when the food arrives, it's mannerly to remove them to avoid knocking over any utensils. Leave your phone in your purse. Instead of texting at the table, try talking at the table – it sounds foreign, but that's what human beings did years ago! Allow your memory to capture the essence of the moment. If you don't want your phone out of sight, suggest you both put your smart phones and devices in the middle of the table –

the first one to use it, has to pay for the meal. When your smart phone battery dies, maybe you can truly start living.

Okay, so your knife blade should be placed on the edge of your plate when not in use and should always face inward. The salad fork, knife and soupspoon are furthest from the main plate than the main course knife, fork and spoon. Dessert utensils are either placed above the main plate or served with dessert.

First things first: say a blessing over your meal and wait until everyone has been served to begin eating. Don't place an entire dinner roll into your mouth; break off bite sizes only. If food is too hot, have a cold beverage with it. On no account spit it out! If you put the food in your mouth, no matter how much you hate it, swallow it. It's rude to take anything out of your mouth that's been put in it except bones, seeds, foods you're allergic to, etc.

Always thank the preparer of the meal, no matter how good or bad the food is. The praise is for the process and displays your gratitude. It's not just about the meal. If the food is really that bad, don't hesitate to discreetly and kindly let the waiter know. Refrain from making a big deal about it. A good rule of thumb is to never insult the one who prepares your food…trust me! Also, make a mental note of what not to order next time, if there is a next time. Follow the pace of your guest and don't finish your meal too soon before or too late after them. Don't *drink* anything with a *spoon*. Unless you are an infant or an ape, don't intentionally play with or make a mess of food. Act like a human and chew with your mouth closed. If you're asked a question while eating, don't answer with food in your mouth; signal that your mouth is full and swallow before speaking. Don't slurp your drink. During restroom breaks, place your napkin in your chair to signify that you are returning, and your fork upside down (prongs down), crossing the knife. When finished with your meal, place your napkin to the left of your dinner plate, and your knife (blade turned inward) and fork should be placed beside each other on the plate diagonally from upper left to lower right.

This may sound like a bunch of nonsense, but a gentlewoman who knows how to formally dine is a gentlewoman with class. You never know when this skill will be useful. It can prove purposeful for romantic dates, business dates and formal dinners. When in the privacy of your own home, relax, put your feet up and enjoy you food how you desire!

The Contemporary Date: You ask; you pay. Think of it like any other activity. If you invited friends over for dinner, you wouldn't expect them to cook. The person who initiates the date is expected to take care of the date. That might be you, or it could be him. Women today generally have more financial freedom than their grandmother's generation did. Besides, there's power in paying your own way. It proves to a man that you're financially secure with or without him. It provides an equal playing field and releases some of the pressure associated with first-time dating. The best way to let us know we aren't getting any at the end of a date is to shake our hand and pay for the bill.

The Traditional Date: <u>Date 1:</u> We pay | <u>Date 2:</u> We pay | <u>Date 3:</u> You offer, but we pay | <u>Date 4:</u> You pay. For some men, letting a Lady foot the bill is an inferiority complex, just like some women take offense to us holding open your door. Let's not make a big deal about this. If we insist on paying, don't hesitate to let it be. Also, don't hesitate to let us know that paying for a meal doesn't entitle us to anything. Some men think that buying dinner means you owe them sex for dessert. Well, they should be arrested for prostitution solicitation. The only thing we've rightfully earned is a thank you. Don't get caught up in the moment and make decisions you'll regret. One good meal shouldn't seal the deal. Don't get overly excited that he took you out for sea bass and wine. If you do decide to give it up for fish and grapes, let it be your decision. It must be a decision that you're comfortable waking up in the morning with.

There exists a difference between a man who spends on you, and a man who invests in you. Figure it out.

Just because he's paid and he pays doesn't mean he thinks you're worth his time. Once you've figured that out, figure this out: Money is easy to get back – time, not so much. It's by far the most valuable resource. Figure it out.

The $15 Date Challenge: Challenge your date to only spend a total of $15 for the entire outing. This forces creativity and thoughtfulness. It can get interesting! It also alleviates any concern we may have about your motives. In all seriousness, a creative date is doper than dinner and a movie. Movie theaters require you to sit still in the dark and be quiet for an hour or two. If a day is organized and specifically tailored to you, it'll be unforgettable. Some of the best dates require lots of thought, not lots of money. Fresh fruit, an early morning hike, the art gallery, change clothes, have a picnic with wine on the beach and then cook what's already in you fridge over sensational conversation that leads far past your bedtime. Don't forget to watch the sunset. Expensive doesn't mean enjoyable. Trust me, try it and enjoy! Just don't be so quick to call home and tell everyone about it. Stay levelheaded with a clear

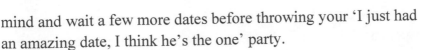

mind and wait a few more dates before throwing your 'I just had an amazing date, I think he's the one' party.

Have you ever felt like you were in love, then you burped and it went away? Don't let those little butterflies in your stomach fool you into thinking you're compatible – it's probably just gas.

Before telling him what you're looking for, let him show you who he is

Sometimes you just have to sit back, watch and observe. People will eventually show you who they are without you saying a word. This doesn't mean to shut down and close off all conversation. It means to be wise about all the information you divulge and when you divulge it. Some people will use your own blueprint against you.

A WOMAN'S INTUITION ISN'T INSECURITY

You know that thought you thought about, but forgot about it because it seemingly came out of *nowhere*? Well, you might want to rethink that. Red flags are conveniently present prior to relationships. Don't ignore them. If you have to go through his phone to see if your relationship is in trouble, your relationship is in trouble. When someone unravels and reveals their true self, you must believe them. There's no need to nag or snoop. Plan your exit, grab the popcorn and enjoy the show.

Be you. Don't show up as your representative. That's the common act of attempting to impress someone with everything that you're not. We'll spend an entire relationship trying to find a person who never existed.

The Long Distance Dater: Long distance relationships are no different than any other relationships in that they both require serious amounts of maturity, effort, creativity, communication, commitment, trust, patience and a plan! There must always be an effective plan in place to see the other again. It's essential to the health of the relationship to manage the anticipation by having a consistent arrangement in place to see your love again. There must also be and end goal. The distance between you must eventually be decreased to his side of the bed–not to sleep in, but to chat of course.

If you can't handle long distance love, you can't handle love, period. Anything worth having is worth working for and love will always be worth the salary.

Long distance relationships aren't the problem; it's the people in them that are the problem. People are afraid of sacrifice. Instead of catching flights, folks would rather *Skype*. Effort is the fuel to take you that extra mile. Distance doesn't ruin a relationship, doubt does. Humans often put the blame on situations, rather then themselves. Excuses are probably *in* this season!

Long distance loving takes some serious sacrifice, and that sacrifice includes you. Don't put *all* the pressure on a man to make all the plans to always come to you. Love is we, not just me–and "we" definitely includes you.

Love is patient, and if you aren't, well then it isn't love. The greatest relationship I've ever been in was a long distance relationship. It tests your strength and character, but the thought of seeing her again was more than enough to hold on. The truest act

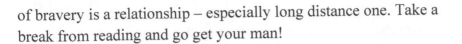

of bravery is a relationship – especially long distance one. Take a break from reading and go get your man!

The Progression: Life is beautiful and busy, but you make time for what's important, period. Your Tuesday's together turn into weekends–weekends turn into sleep-ins. All is well! He's such a gentleman. All your girlfriends call him by his nickname. And although you've been dating for some time, you turn into a teen when his name appears in your caller I.D. His voice feels like the only blanket in the house in the wintertime. The feeling is like sipped mellowed rare whiskey, neat. You daydreamed about the taste of his intimacy. Slow down. Sometimes it's best to imagine.

Courtship is dating for the purposes of marriage. It's the period of the pursuit where a couple develops a romantic relationship. Maybe you're prepared to progress the bond, but how do you know if a man is? Many times a woman will look for cues to indicate whether we're ready to take things to the next level. She'll read tips in magazines or watch tutorials online. There's no need to go on a scavenger hunt to determine if a man is ready for a relationship. Just ask. Don't underestimate the power of asking a basic question. And don't ask your friends, or his friends, or a relationship coach–go directly to the source and ask him.

Inquiring about the progress of a relationship doesn't have to be a daunting task. If you're with someone who truly cares for you, why are you afraid to ask that person about your future together? Quit looking for symbols and secret signs and just have an adult conversation for once. If you desire something serious, you're going to have to put yourself out there and talk about it. If you wait for him or for the right time, you might be waiting forever. "Someday" isn't on your calendar. If you were hungry and desired food, you wouldn't wait for someone to offer you a plate. Treat this scenario no differently. But be prepared for any reaction. When we say we don't know what we want, we don't want you. Indecision is non-negotiable. You can't force a *time limit* on such a serious decision, but a responsible man who dates a wonderful woman knows within a reasonable amount of time if he wants to advance the relationship. Maybe we're just comfortable with exactly the way things are. Maybe we're not ready. Perhaps we'll agree with plans for a future. Respect our decision because it's our decision. Just react accordingly. If bringing up marriage will scare us off, perhaps you should bring up marriage. You have a right to state your expectations, but you don't have the right to hold us accountable for expectations we haven't discussed and agreed upon. There are no guarantees in dating.

THE NBA IS A GREAT EXAMPLE OF RELATIONSHIPS – THE MAJORITY OF PEOPLE WITHOUT A RING IN THREE TO FIVE YEARS GET RELEASED OR TRADED

Here's a dose of reality: Your boyfriend of ten years *probably* won't be marrying you. To hell with his analogies about waiting to test drive before making the purchase. A Lady isn't a vehicle–she's a Lady. How many times will he be allowed to taste the fish before throwing it back into the sea? People don't get PhD's prior to preschool. Privileges are escalated when vows are elevated. Expecting a single Lady to act married is like refusing to sign a lease and not paying a dime of rent, but expecting a house key, fridge full of food plus a few luxury cars in the garage. People have to *pay* to play and the *price* for your whole heart, body, being and mind is marriage. Your entirety is a luxury! There should be certain benefits reserved and boundaries set for marriage. You determine what those boundaries are. The ball might be in our court but, you're the referee. Call the fouls and regulate the game or we might play right through it. This is exactly why you shouldn't act married if you're not. You're not a wife – you're an unpaid intern.

Don't play dumb and don't turn a blind eye because he's beautiful and his stroke is good. Hold your partner accountable. Stop letting average Joes tell you how *busy* they are. The President is **busy** and he takes his wife on monthly dates. You really don't have to settle for the foolishness you settle for in a relationship. Stop allowing it! Dates don't stop after dating. Anything valuable requires maintenance or it'll fall apart. Since we like to compare you to cars, we should know best that if you expect something to perform well, you must treat it well. Well, the same goes for relationships. The more you put into it, the more you get out of it. What's it going to be?

Ultimately, your dating rules and decisions are your own. Some prefer swinging and some prefer open relationships. Whatever you decide, ensure you're being treated the way you want to be treated.

The Decision: "I've got your back." "I believe in you." I'm proud of you." If you don't hear these words in your relationship, you might be in the wrong one. A Lady's support makes a man want to take over the world. And our support makes you want to do the same. Not just financial support. He might've bought you a sexy car, but without your own drive, you're not *that* sexy. We're attracted to ambition, and relationships work best when couples are supportive of each other's goals.

DON'T PUT YOUR PURPOSE ON HOLD FOR PENIS

Lust has a capacity. Love is bottomless. You eventually come down from the high of something solely steamy and desire something fulfilling. You adjust to lust. A spark isn't enough to ignite the flame to cause the fire that burns throughout a hot relationship. At this point, sex isn't enough. Being handsome and funny aren't enough. Being equally yoked is the goal. A woman at 40 might think of having children – A man at 40 might think of dating children. Relationship evaluations are a necessary tool to determine if both of your standards are being met and if you're where you want to be. Before you try to fix anything, sit back and decide if it's even worth fixing. If your relationship doesn't inspire you and you don't inspire it, you're wasting each other's time. It's unwise to continue dating if standards go unmet. It's mature to discontinue dating if you've come to the realization that you're ill equipped for the journey.

If your relationship consists of consistently fighting to make it work, you're probably in the wrong one.

The Breakup: Severing ties with someone is something that most people will have to do at some point in their lives. The unfortunate fact is people often mistake someone that was placed in their lives for a specific reason, as a soul mate. It happens all the time. They're so eager for love that they reassign people's purpose and positions in their lives and latch onto the innocent bystander. Then you find out that the man you married was placed in your life to be the friend that introduced you to your husband. Oops!

The problem isn't always coming to grips with the fact that you have to say goodbye, but how to actually say it. What's proper protocol when it comes to a departure? Using technology to sever ties is common, but certainly cowardly. We all need to get back to the forgotten art of saying, "So long."

When the love story ends, breaking up isn't hard to do. To toss your insignificant other to the curb, you'll need a few courtesies to keep in mind:

- **Do it yourself.** You can't send someone else to do your dirty work. It's the perfect way to burn a bridge. You got yourself into this mess, now get yourself out.

- **Face reality.** You can't go around ignoring calls and cutting off communication without breaking up first. Be a gentlewoman. If you're unhappy, then say so. Ignoring red flags in relationships is like ignoring red traffic lights. Prepare for a wreck.

- **Be upfront.** Dropping hints that you're no longer interested is unnecessary. Being direct and open will produce the best results, although results may vary.

- **Be honest.** Falling out of love is just as uncomfortable as falling in–falling is never comfortable. But attempting to make your significant other hate you is childlike. Immaturity went out of style with insecurity.

-**Get over it.** Keep your, "Ooh girl, let me tell you about him," comments to yourself. Perhaps he treats her better because she's better for him. Going off isn't moving on. To consistently and publicly display hatred for an ex says much more about you than him. You're over a former fling when you can smile seeing him with someone else. Just because you didn't work out doesn't mean they won't work out. If you're not careful, your anger toward your ex will transition into anger toward the next. Forgiveness isn't just for him; it's for you. Besides, dating is just an elimination process – quit acting like your past owes you something.

When you do decide to breakup, breakup gracefully with class. Saying goodbye doesn't have to be at his eulogy. Let's settle this like gentlewomen and gentlemen.

And let's be honest. Aren't you glad certain relationships didn't work out? Sometimes the words, "It's over," are exactly what you need to say or hear. Breakups are often blessings that lead you to the person you're intended to be with. Say thank you! Some relationships are just meant for a season. Quit letting people make it snow in your summertime. Besides, if he's dumb enough to walk away, be smart enough to let him go. The end of a relationship might be the beginning of your life.

Be wise enough to thank God for not giving you some of the things you asked for and gracious enough to enjoy what He gave you instead.

We all want what we can't have once it's gone because it's then we realize how good it was. If you're going to move on, you need to move on completely. That doesn't make you mean spirited - it makes you an ex.

A nice way to move on is to create a zero access zone. Delete your ex from all social networking accounts and even use the block feature if need be. Don't respond to any attempted communication. If harassment is involved, change your number. If you don't want to change your cell phone number, simply utilize the block button.

If your ex calls from different numbers, file a police report. Direct all emails to spam and cut communication completely. There really is no excuse to not let go. Don't leave to see if someone will chase after you. If you leave, leave because you aren't coming back. If he's still in your life, it's because a small part of you wants him to be. You're in complete control of whom you allow in your lives.

It's foolish to pay the price for the experience and neglect the lesson. Learn from the mistakes you dated. Otherwise, your ex-boyfriend will be your next boyfriend.

SECOND CHANCES: You don't give second chances when they're beneath your morals, values and ethics. You have to know the difference between settling and being outright unrealistic. Settling is doing something you wouldn't normally do just to satisfy a selfish temporary desire. Being unrealistic is demanding a perfect man or requiring a checklist that you don't yet meet yourself. Provide second chances when you feel a real interest in someone. If something silly turned you off and your disgust is unmerited, then really think about what's important. Bad breath turns some women off to no return. Others realize some mouthwash will temporarily rectify the simple issue and a trip to the dentist will solve it. On the other hand, if someone seriously turns you off, you're not obligated to keep him around. No hard feelings.

On the contrary, his love might make dinner on the couch feel like a five-star restaurant. The measure of a great relationship is the ability to fall in love with the same person daily. You don't get sick of being around him, but you're sick when he's not around. He's the specific answer to your prayers. He even mentioned introducing you to his parents. You're prepared for a lifetime.

Meeting the Parents: Meeting his family? Well, congratulations. But meeting mom doesn't mean marriage. Some cats bring strays home. Here's what to generally expect: His dad is easy. He thinks you're pretty and probably won't say much–small talk and smiles. He might keep the conversation going just to see where your head is. His mom is another story. She can potentially be more critical. My advice for you is to just be yourself. You're not marrying his mom. It'd be great for her to like you, but so what if she doesn't. If the mother is a kind and neutral woman and dislikes you–maybe, just maybe you might want to evaluate yourself. If you pass your humble self-evaluation check, then her disliking you is her problem.

The same goes for your parents. If your parents unjustifiably dislike your potential spouse, that's a problem they'll have to deal with on their own. If you're an adult capable of making adult decision, never allow your mom to dictate or control your happy love life. No man in his right mind will want to put up with a crazy mother in the way. If you're a mother reading this, you are not your daughter. You don't choose her dates. You don't choose her husband. You raised your child...now let her be an adult. Good day to you!

It's not against any law to dislike future/current in-laws. People are people and not every family member is pleasant. The goal is to always maintain cordiality, but don't feel obligated to invite them over every weekend.

Now, let's get on to the next phase and best phase.
The Marriage: Some want it. We all need it, but we don't all understand it. Do you know what it means to say I love you? Do

you realize what you're saying? You're agreeing to never give up; care more for that person than for yourself; not wanting what you don't have; have no ego or arrogance; not forcing yourself on that person; not always being "me first;" never flying off the handle; keeping no score of wrongdoing; never reveling when that person grovels. Instead, you're saying you're to take pleasure in the flowering of truth, put up with anything, trust God always, always look for the best, never look back, but keep going to the end. Now ask yourself, do you really love him? Does he really love you?

Have you gotten so used to saying "we" that you no longer desire to say "I" anymore. Love isn't just those butterflies in your stomach. It isn't about getting your way. Love is about service. It's about taking unpopular routes and not always doing what you feel like doing for the benefit of another. Love makes self-centeredness the enemy. It's the most selfless act you can commit. It's easy to be loved, but not always easy to love. To say "I love you" says, "I know exactly who you are and I accept you still. I will lay down my very own life for you." There's nothing more comforting than that. That's what a marriage is. May that very love sustain you, flow through your bloodline and shake the earth at its very core. **NOTE**: Never allow someone to use love against you. Love isn't rape. Love isn't pain. Love isn't forced. Love is beautiful and it's natural. Have discernment. Know the difference.

"Pray for your marriage before you get into it." - *Grandma Frettie Jackson*

Let no one push you into getting married. It's a lifetime decision that requires prayer, not pressure. In making the honorable decision to unite your love into one, be certain that you've selected the proper suitor. If there are ever any doubts, then don't say I do.

Don't go into a marriage with any uncertainty. It's better to break an engagement than it is to break a lifetime. Marriage is a fresh start. Don't come into marriage saying, "This is how it's done because this is how we did it growing up." You must cleave to your spouse and honor your new life together. It's about redemption. The past no longer matters, so don't bring up past mistakes. If you're not prepared to accept this, you're not prepared for marriage.

Marriage is a mirror. It's a confrontation with yourself that shows you who you are by revealing the depth of your faults and strengths. People often run from their faults, but marriage won't allow that. It might the first time your flaws directly affect you. You have the ability to ruin your own life through marriage. Many don't understand this truth and end up blaming their spouse in divorce court. If you humbly submit to your marriage, it will make you the best possible version of yourself. This goes both ways for woman and man.

Speak highly of your spouse. Never belittle your partner to anyone. Keep your business in-house. God comes first and your spouse comes right after. Your kids come next. If your foundation isn't in order, nothing else will be. This includes your marriage and your family. A marriage needs way more planning than a wedding–don't believe the hype. Marriage won't be perfect because nothing is, but marriage is the most beautiful honor in the world. There will be seasons of summers and seasons of winters. You will fall out of like with your spouse because emotions come and go. This isn't a time to be weak and reconsider the union. It's a time to be strong and get back to that joyous place. You have to be intentional in marriage. You must make the decision to love when you don't feel like it or feel the other person deserves it. Sometimes you'll be the strong one, and other times you'll need your spouse to be. But when you don't trust God to meet your deep needs, you transfer the expectation to your marriage and set it up for failure. Spiritual needs can't be met by human beings. Just like a laptop computer must stay connected to its power source, so too do couples. People don't have enough to rely on their own supply. Keep your marriage connected to your power source.

Ignore those statistics meant to scare you. Statistics shouldn't just reflect unmarried women; they should reflect unmarried women who have no desire to be married. Not every woman's fairytale ends in a white dress. Many women are just fine with that. You can be disinterested in the idea of marriage, but don't discount it. When people say marriage is just a piece of paper, I tell them their money, degree(s), job contract, laws and U.S. Constitution are too. A dating relationship isn't until death do you part – it's until someone better comes along or something breaks you apart. Having a spouse with benefits is different than having a friend with benefits. Place whatever nametag or title you want on it, but you're single unless you're married. This fact **does not** excuse disrespect in any other form of commitment.

Sexual Symmetry: You better balance your work life with your married life. That master's degree isn't going to provide you with a subtle neck kiss or make love to you.

Flirting after marriage: Flirting is harmless as long as you are. Marriage shouldn't take away your personality and glow. If you are naturally personable, keep being yourself. However, understand the difference between a smile and a lascivious wink. Don't do or say anything that your partner wouldn't be comfortable with or would place you in harm's way.

The Bottom Line: Marriage isn't a joke – people are. Love doesn't hurt – people do. Figure it out and live life.

The Divorce: This should be your last result after exhausting all possible options to reconcile. The fact of the matter is that sometimes you marry the wrong person. Or you could be the wrong person that the right person married.

LOVE FELL IN LUST WITH HOPE

Divorce should never be your first option. It shouldn't even be on your radar. The option to divorce should be hidden in a place so deep that your spouse has to go to the darkest place to access and trigger it. Just as you should pray before you make the decision to marry, pray before you make the decision to divorce. Whatever the decision, don't beat yourself up over it. Handle the process like a gentlewoman and move on with life as best you can. It will get better! You're not damaged goods. Life isn't over. God still loves you.

Happily Ever After: Is there such a thing? Well, it's all about perspective. Contentment is the real "happily ever after." Being content in a relationship doesn't mean lowering your standards. Keep your standards–they're meant to protect you. But keep your mind in the process, because you've lost it if you think you'll ever have a relationship without problems. Happily ever after is a decision because happiness is a choice. It isn't dependent upon situational variables. Your happiness is happening right now...unless you chose not to see it. That doesn't mean to be naive. It means to stop focusing on the little bit that's wrong with him and enjoy what's right, or get left.

Relationships are flawed because you are. People are. People will always have problems, but if he loves you and the good outweighs the bad, learn contentment. Never become so invested in the perception of someone else's joy that you fail to notice your own.

The best relationships often occur by accident...don't be afraid to get into an accident. Be open. Be ready.

Don't be afraid of getting hurt. Instead, be afraid of losing all common sense, settling and failing to see the obvious. Every time you get into a relationship, there's risk of heartbreak. Every time you get into a car, there's risk of a fatal accident. You're afraid of a relationship, but you're not afraid to drive? Common sense is a seat belt. You might experience pain in a wreck, but the impact is less damaging. Love won't hurt you, but people will. We're flawed. Go ahead and reserve a space in your heart for disappointment, but enjoy life, still.

Dating will never be successful without vulnerability. If you desire something serious, you're going to have to put yourself out there. Commitment scares us just as much as it scares you. Understand when a risk is worth it and select wisely. Submission is permission to be vulnerable. Whatever we give a good woman, she'll make greater, including us. Whatever you give a good man, he'll make greater, including you. Drive safely.

Interlude
Gentlemen's Section

Gentlemen's Section: *Man Cave*

Let's be honest, men are reading this book. Whether they sneak a peak while their girlfriend is away, or they want to see what all the hype is about – a man is reading this section right now.

This brief interlude serves as a summary of what men need to know about this book.

o   A secure woman isn't waiting around for you to date her – she's living life. Next time you look up, she'll be married…and pregnant…and happy. OK, maybe not pregnant, or married for that matter, but she'll be happily living life without you. As men, we feel like our money has to be right and all things in place before we take that next step. But someday isn't on any calendar. The most underrated moment is now! You know she's the right one when you display unnecessary resistance. If you don't make your move, someone gladly will. Don't get so caught up "living life" that you have to learn to live with regrets. A Lady who catches onto her worth only puts up with the bull for so long. Get right or get left.

o   One of the cleverest acts a woman commits is acting like she doesn't know…she does. Women somehow know everything, so know that she knows…she just hasn't said anything, yet.

o   Stop taking women on emotional journeys if you're unprepared to accompany them for the ride. Sometimes she wasn't "crazy" until you drove her to be. She was cool until she met you. Now she's emotionally connected and invested from all the sex, lies and empty promises. Her emotional pain could've been manifested in her sexuality. She was easy to smash, but you smashed her soul…genocide. Your thrusts hit her scars, reopening closed wounds. You're actually the crazy one for

248

pulling a disappearing act and thinking she wouldn't react this way. FYI: Some folks are crazy without warrant. Please disregard if this is the case.

- Chivalry doesn't stop after dating. We get her, then forgot how we got her and do the bare minimum to keep her. If you opened the door for her on date one, open the door for her on date 101. The more you pour into her, the more you'll get out of her. That's what a healthy relationship is.

- If you paid full price and got half service, you'd complain too. It's not *nagging* when a good woman won't settle for a half-assed version of a man. Relationships are careers and folks are lying on their application. A resume shouldn't only reflect what you've done, but what you intend to do. Deliver on your promises or be fired. False advertising is illegal. **NOTE**: "Crazy." "Nag." "Unrealistic." Stop hurling these insults at women with common sense and just be a better man.

- An uninterested Lady isn't playing hard to get – she's uninterested. Be gone. This includes all street harassment and cat calling.

- All women don't love flowers. But it's the fact you were thinking of her is the gesture she loves. Find a creative and thoughtful way to let her know she crossed your mind with more than a text message.

- If your Lady is beautiful other men will notice. This shouldn't make you insecure…it should make you smile. Relax. Another man looking at your Lady is a compliment. Another man lurking after your Lady is disrespect. Understand the difference.

- You'll find her blueprint in this book, but no two women are quite the same. Ladies aren't monolithic. Take real time to get to know her specifically. Learn what makes her laugh and what makes her angry. Study her actions and reactions. Memorize the curves on her lips. Both of them.

o She's just like you.

If you think I'm ruining your "game," then you absolutely have none. Besides, game with no real follow-up is a weak plan. If you make her weak in the knees, then you should be prepared to catch her when she falls. Listen, you're being replaced by degrees and dogs. It's time to step up and be the man that I know you've been called to be. None of this is intended to sell you out or demean you. It's intended to make you better. You're worthy of that and so is she. This is rooted in honesty and love. Gentlewomen deserve gentlemen and anything less should never be tolerated. In order to get into Harvard University, you must meet Harvard University's standards. In order to receive a gold medal, you must train, run and win the race. You wouldn't put a $100 bid on a five million dollar home. A gentlewoman is greater than all of these things. Is she not more valuable than this?

"HER CLOTHES ARE WELL-MADE AND ELEGANT, AND SHE ALWAYS FACES TOMORROW WITH A SMILE. WHEN SHE SPEAKS SHE HAS SOMETHING WORTHWHILE TO SAY, AND SHE ALWAYS SAYS IT KINDLY. SHE KEEPS AN EYE ON EVERYONE IN HER HOUSEHOLD, AND KEEPS THEM ALL BUSY AND PRODUCTIVE. HER CHILDREN RESPECT AND BLESS HER; HER HUSBAND JOINS IN WITH WORDS OF PRAISE: MANY WOMEN HAVE DONE WONDERFUL THINGS, BUT YOU'VE OUTCLASSED THEM ALL!"–
PROVERBS 31:25-29, THE MESSAGE

Shut Up and Train

Shut Up and Train: *The Gauntlet*

Wellness is more than just a clean bill of health from a doctor. To be healthy is to have symmetry between your mind, body and soul. This isn't some awkward spiritual talk. You're more than just a body. The soul and mind are well connected.

A greater focus on the body than on the soul is useless. What good are great breasts if behind them is an ugly heart? Don't workout your mind and fail to workout your body. If you feed your body and neglect your soul, you'll still be hungry. When you take care of your entire being, all other areas of life will fall into place. You'll be a better worker, a better lover and a better woman. And you'll never have to stress about going on a stupid little date! Gentlemen will be options–*just don't treat us like options*. Good health is where you find great balance. Never neglect you.

DIET.
Some say healthy food is too expensive – I say healthy food is cheaper than a hospital bill. Jerri Evans says: *"I'm healthy; I work out; I eat vegetables; I buy a lot of organic food,"* or my favorite, *"I buy the most expensive products because they're the best,"* are comments I hear from clients before we truly evaluate their health regimen. The first thing we do at Turning Natural is to instill that good health starts on your plate. Once you tackle that, the rest is a breeze.

You're in for a real treat! I've enlisted my good friend, Health and Wealth Specialist, Everett Frampton to provide three of his private recipes for delectable snacks that don't compromise in taste or nutrients:

Tasty recipes are gluten-free and dairy-free for your pleasure:

Three easy-to-make healthy recipes:

Protein Ball Pops*: Makes 20 – 30 balls*
-2 cups of Almond Butter (peanut butter)
-2 cups of organic honey
-8 cups of Quaker Oats oatmeal
-24 scoops of a dairy-free, gluten-free,
Non-GMO protein (standard scooper in
most product containers).
-3/4 cup ground flax seeds
-1/2 cup dried blueberries (optional)

Directions:
With hands and gloves - mix ingredients,
while adding only as-needed water or
almond milk until mixture can be hand
rolled into a golf ball size. Place in a
tray or sheet and keep refrigerated. After
the first 2 hours, they're ready for you to
enjoy!
* You can enjoy before/after exercise, or
a snack in-between meals.

Frampton's on Kauai*: Serves 6*
-10 slices of turkey bacon
(sliced/chopped up)
-2 lbs. of salmon (7 ounces each slice)
-1 onion sliced
-7 cloves of garlic
-1 ounce of vegetable stock
-Kosher salt to taste / cayenne pepper to taste
-tsp. of ghee butter
-8 sprigs of fresh thyme
-6 cage-free organic eggs
-2 bunches of kale - washed/chopped down

Directions:
2 pans needed. Sauté the onions, garlic, turkey bacon and thyme in ghee butter. Add kale. Cook until kale is to your liking. Sear salmon with ingredient seasonings. Fry 1 egg per person medium sunny side-up. Place kale on the pate first. Stack with a salmon portions and top off with fried egg on top.
* This is a great light and healthy breakfast.

Turducken Pan Seared Meat
Ball/Wraps: *Serves 4-6*
-1 lb. ground turkey
-1 lb. ground chicken
-1 lb. ground duck
-1 medium onion
-8 cloves garlic
-8 sprigs thyme minced
-2 tsp. olive oil
-kosher salt and/or cayenne pepper to
taste
-1 head of butter lettuce
-mango chutney (jar)
-1 bunch of minced parsley
-1 red onion minced
<u>Directions</u>:
Make meatball portions, sear them in a
sauté pan and finish them in oven. Serve
meatballs wrapped in butter lettuce,
topped with mango chutney, parsley and
fresh red onions.
* <u>This is perfect for lunch or dinner!</u>

-Please enjoy.

HEALTHY MEALS WITHOUT EXERCISE HELP YOU LOOK GOOD WITH CLOTHES ON – HEALTHY MEALS WITH EXERCISE HELPS YOU LOOK GOOD WITH YOUR CLOTHES OFF.

EXERCISE.
For some, the most difficult workout is exercising common sense. Avoiding exercise because you got your hair done is a tragedy. There are too many excuses used to get out of going to the gym: *It's too expensive, I'll do it next year; I don't have time.* Quit waiting to exhale. Instead of holding your breath in bikinis, hold up weights at the gym. Some people take advantage of good health. It's like the electricity going out – you don't think about it when it's on, but if it goes out, it's the end of the world! Be proactive. Don't wait too late to be healthy. Photoshop isn't a gym. It's digital plastic surgery.

You don't have to take my word for it. I've enlisted the help of Celebrity Trainer and Goal Coach, Rahman Ray Grayson, a.k.a. Mr. Shut Up And Train. He's got your back…butt…legs and abs, too!

Rahman Ray Grayson, a.k.a. Mr. Shut Up And Train
Celebrity Trainer | Goal Coach | President & CEO of AEIM Fitness

We've become a microwave society. We want quick and fast results and solutions to long-term problems. You don't gain weight overnight and you won't lose it overnight. You don't develop unhealthy habits overnight and we won't shake these unhealthy habits overnight either. It's about long-term adaption of healthy lifestyle practices. Small changes day-by-day ultimately help a woman lead a healthier life.

Dispel the quick diet myth.
I don't want clients shedding 40 pounds in 2-3 weeks. It's all coming right back. I'd rather it be a slower process. I teach them how to live healthy: Eat clean, work hard, stay disciplined and you'll get to where you need to be.

Not everyone feels like this type of lifestyle is a necessity. Maybe every once in a while, but life gets busy. What's the importance of fitness and its direct benefits?
The importance is fitness is a long-term quality of life! Plus, you look good, feel good and have greater self-confidence. There are many benefits to healthy living that far outweigh the instant gratification you may get from an unhealthy night or divulging in unhealthy eating or drugs. Your body is a temple. You've got to take care of your temple because last time I checked, that's the only one that you get!

The desire to indulge is human. Embrace it. I'm a fan of living life and enjoying life. Live healthy, indulge when it's time to indulge and then get right back to living healthy again. Let's not try to do the opposite by living a lifestyle of indulgence, live healthy for a week or two and then get back to a lifestyle of indulgence. I preach the 80/20-Rule. Eighty percent of the time, eat clean, whole, nutritious foods from the earth. Drink your water and green tea. I'm a big fan of black coffee. It's an antioxidant source as well as a source of energy. Eighty percent of the time, that's what I want you doing. The other twenty percent, whatever you want. It's simple math! You don't cheat every weekend, but two out of 10 meals can be something unhealthy. Don't take this suggestion too far. It's unwise to be a weekend warrior who lives healthy throughout the week. Your body can't truly recover from that. You think you can because when you're younger, your metabolism is revved up due to age being on your side. But when you're older, your lifestyle likely isn't as active and that behavior can shut you down. And that's why 25-40-year-olds begin paying attention to all those infomercials, gadgets and magic pills.

You might say, "I've always been able to eat this and stay in shape," but your body is a machine. All machines are pre-equipped with what it needs to stay revved up. Over a span of one's lifestyle, if you don't keep that machine fine tuned, then your machine will start working slower, and slower and slower. And you start putting more stuff in your machine that's not cranking your machine – instead, it's slowing it down.

And that's often what happens – your metabolism is slow, body is getting fat and people think not eating is the key. Wrong again! If you don't put fuel in a car, after a while it does what? Even before the car stops, it slows down and functions stop working. The car may still run and you think it's OK because it cranks, but underneath, certain things just aren't working the way they should. Sooner or later that car will die out.

Life catches up to you.

What to avoid?
Alcohol is a huge problem many of my adult clients don't want to address. Oftentimes, they consume alcohol to offset underlying issues. As a personal trainer, I also serve as a goal coach. When we dig a little deeper, together we find out why a person may turn to alcohol at certain times of the night, or the day, or the week or

their life. We get to the bottom of the stressful satiations they're trying to mask.

What are some quick, simple and effective routines that can be done at home with no equipment regardless of body type?
If you only have so much time and can fit in certain exercises, I recommend:

- o *Burpees: Great total body exercise*
- o *Walking Lunges: great for legs, glutes, quads and hamstrings. Whenever you're working bigger muscle groups, you're burning more calories.*
- o *Push-ups: Any variation will work your chest as well as your triceps.*

Final words.
When you're dating, you have to check a person's commitment to health and fitness. A lot of my clients I've converted to healthier lifestyle will say, "If the person I'm dating or the person I'm with isn't committed to health and fitness, I don't see how I can raise kids with this person. We'll be teaching two totally different things." Make sure you're equally yoked. Make a commitment to living a healthy lifestyle.

You will reach your goal! I've had clients who've been overweight their whole life and have never been comfortable with their bodies. They finally buy into fitness and healthy eating between 25 and 30 years old and finally realize it's attainable for anybody. When you work hard, there really are no limitations to what you can do. Find what works for you. Make no excuses. Hair is no excuse. If a woman is confident about the way her body looks, by default, she's going to take care of her hair. If you get your body where you want it, you'll make sure your hair looks good even if it takes an extra 15 to 30 minutes preparation time because everything else looks good. Shut up and train!

2-Minute Abs Workout (2 sets)

- Crunches
- Rocky Balboas aka Boxer Sit-ups
- Toe Touches
- V-Sits aka Vertical sit-ups
- Muffin Tops aka Core Twists

+ Set 1: 25 reps of each exercise | Take a 30 second rest

+ Set 2: 20 reps of each exercise

Rahman Ray Grayson, a.k.a. Mr. Shut Up And Train | Celebrity Personal Trainer | Goal Coach | MrShutUpAndTrain.com

Disclaimer: *All material provided is provided for informational or educational purposes only. The Bereolaesque Group, Total Fit team nor anyone associated with Mr. Shut Up & Train will be responsible or liable for any injury sustained while exercising at your home, gym or elsewhere. Consult a physician regarding the applicability of any opinions or recommendations with respect to your symptoms or medical condition.*

A gentleman's appreciation for the feminine form is more sophisticated. That subtle jiggle in your sundress tastes better than wine. Your curves shouldn't get on your nerves. What's beautiful road scenery without a few twist and turns? Embrace your shape. We certainly do. The goal isn't to be thin; the goal is to be healthy! Please say yes to the sundress!

REST.

Good sleep has been compared to good sex, but the majority of people aren't getting much of either. For a younger and more ambitious generation, staying awake has become an increasingly fashionable topic to brag about. The damage done to the body due to a lack of rest can kill you before you get to enjoy what you've worked hard for. Rest is a gift from God. Even He rested after creating earth (Genesis 2:2). What makes you think you don't have to?

Insomnia isn't sexy–it's an illness. The only bags that look good on a Lady are under her arms, not under her eyes. A restless woman is a rest-less woman. Working tirelessly isn't always the solution. The human mind, body and spirit are like a webpage that times out–it requires refreshing. Sleep replenishes and reinvigorates you. Beauty rest isn't some catchphrase reserved for the high maintenance. When you don't get rest, it shows. And overtime, it can decrease your quality of life.

Set a schedule. Go to bed earlier and you can wake up earlier. There's always work to do. When you're dead and gone, there will still be work to do. So while you're awake do your best, but God will do the rest while you rest. You can't outwork God. Take your butt to bed and sleep like your life depends on it…because it does.

Despite how it looks, no one has it all. But it's not about having it all; it's about successfully balancing what you do have. If you decide to stay home and raise kids while you're husband works, it doesn't devalue you in any way. If you want to be a career woman, it doesn't make you any greater than a stay-at-home wife. Whether you want to be a workaholic or balance work and family, you choose your priorities. Never neglect your health chasing success.

Idoroenyi Amanam, M.D.
Physician

Gentlewomen,

I'm a physician and contrary to popular belief, I would love to see less of you. My job is to keep you alive when you fall ill, but more importantly, impart advice that keeps you in good health (and out of the emergency room). If you've had the good fortune to pick up this book and open to this chapter, I can deduce that you're a pleasant, curious and logical woman of the world. I bet you make appointments and keep them, deliver food to your friends who are new moms, heed traffic signs, and only bring 8 items to the 10 items-or-less counter. This is you managing the vicissitudes of life. Unfortunately, I can't say that your stellar life management skills will translate into you making the right choices about your health. What are those choices you ask? Read on…

Preventative medicine is more important than ever – this is not new to you intelligent reader. However, the hardest part of my job is convincing you to follow my recommendations and advice aimed at…prevention. I'm regularly dismayed and baffled at my inability to convince you, who is otherwise healthy, that it's imperative that you take your blood pressure pills. I sort of get it - you have no symptoms and there is no physical evidence of disease - thank goodness. But I'm not in the business of prescribing unnecessary medications or needless advice, so if I prescribe it, you should probably take it *as directed.*

Take Camille, a gregarious 42 year-old woman who meticulously has cared for her skin looks to be just shy of 35. She appears healthy and generally is (based on routine physicals and tests), but her uncontrolled blood pressure will kill her. She can't see it. So to her it doesn't exist. I see cases like Camille's daily. Many people's understanding of illness is the bacterial infectious disease model. You contract an illness. Shortly thereafter you have symptoms. Then, you have treatment that resolves symptoms and cures the illness. The problem is that model only fits for a portion of illnesses. The top two causes of death for women: Heart Disease and Cancer (via 2010 CDC statistics) definitely do not fit the infectious disease paradigm.

My job is to convince my patients that those statistics are real and the mundane advice that doctors give their patients are actually worthwhile. So what's that advice?

Heart disease the leading cause of death in women is an all-encompassing description of any disease that affects the cardiovascular system. This includes coronary artery disease, high blood pressure, and structural heart diseases and irregular heartbeats. I still haven't figured out how to make my advice exciting. It's the same that you'll hear from more famous professionals like Dr. Sanjay Gupta or Dr. Mehmet Oz. I'd like to think I'm much more captivating than Mehmet to convince you to eat a low fat- high fiber diet, exercise at least 30 minutes a session five times a week, limit alcohol consumption and abstain from smoking. But who am I kidding. We're inundated with valuable information over television, radio and the Internet that by the time I get my opportunity you've become apathetic to this news. Even so, if you don't follow my advice you increase your chances of acquiring heart disease.

Cancer is a very complex disease process that affects a variety of organs but to put it simply it is uncontrolled cell growth. Though cancer originally named by Hippocrates in 400BC has been known to medicine for a very long time, we have just begun to really understand the complicacy of it all. Though we've made significant advances, we are still trying to find better tools to treat cancers. Until then, we have to rely on screening and prevention of cancer.

The American Cancer Society does a fantastic job of bringing awareness to a variety of cancers. I mean what other organization can convince men, with high levels of testosterone that are paid millions to physically demolish each other on Sundays, that pink socks and gloves in October is the cool thing to do? Though billions of dollars are raised annually to assist in screening and prevention of a variety of cancers, we still lose half of our cancer deaths per year to preventable causes (via report released by AACR '2010).

Lung cancer to me is especially frustrating… the most common killer of cancers among women (4 out of 5 are caused by tobacco). The key is to not smoke. I know it may be difficult for a woman who thinks it's cute to smoke in her black little dress to stop smoking. But we have so much proven data that you should. I'm definitely not the first person to say that smoking kills. But it just really does. I'll also add that it makes your breath stink and decreases your ability to discern between flavors.

There is no consensus in the medical community regarding lung cancer screening and currently it is not routinely done. At the age of 50, you should have started you breast cancer screening with mammograms at least every two years and should have been screened for colon cancer with a colonoscopy (frequency every ten years). Those lung, breast and colon cancer death rates are not static and I'm confident those numbers will improve for the better.

My recommendations are very general and superficial considering the subject matter of this book. You should see a medical professional in order to receive expert assistance regarding your health. Depending on the specialty of the health care provider, you may be presented with slightly different recommendations. My keys to survival are simple. Build a great relationship with your doctor so they can tailor their knowledge to your unique life experience. Live a healthy life. Be in touch with your body…

Most sincerely,
Idoroenyi Amanam, MD

BREAST SELF-EXAM

All adult women are encouraged to check their breasts and perform a self-exam once a month. The best time to perform the exam is three to five days after your monthly cycle to ensure your breasts aren't as lumpy or tender.

Many cases of breast cancer are discovered by women noticing unusual changes and of course, paying a visit to their doctor. The earlier that breast cancer is detected, the better the chance you have at beating this thing. Here's a quick guide to the self-exam:

STEP 1

Lay on your back. Now put your right hand behind your head and use your left three middle fingers to trace your right breast. Repeat the process with your left hand above your head.

STEP 2

Next, stand in front of a mirror and relax. Be at peace. Place your arms to the side and look at your breasts for anything visibly abnormal. Keep an eye out for any changes in shape, any dimpling or swelling of the skin. Repeat the same with hands in the air. Place your palms on hips firmly so that your chest muscles flex. Look for any noticeable changes on either one side. Last, squeeze the nipples and check for crust or discharge.

Please consult a physician for medical advice upon finding anything out of the ordinary. There's no such thing as overreaction or an inappropriate inquiry when it comes to your health. Do not rely solely on self-examinations for detection. Seek medical instruction from a doctor.

King James Version

King James Version: Faith

I don't believe our actions alone determine our place in the afterlife, I believe our faith does. Belief is a powerful behavior. What you believe is what controls your actions. It's the core of who you are. But our bodies bind us. Most people's scope is limited to their senses. If they can't see it, touch it, hear it, taste it or smell it, then they just don't believe it. What satisfies the human senses is what's real to them. Anything else is imagination. It's just a dream.

Dreams are often buried by reality and reality often deters some from even dreaming. There's a generation of people who had to give up their dreams to work nine-to-five jobs and provide for their families. Many of those employed aren't working jobs that fulfill their passion. There are teachers who wish they were cooks, and cooks who truly have a passion for painting. The world is so mixed up with people in the wrong careers who had to compromise their passion for paychecks. Well how much can a job pay you to give up on your dreams?

Then, you have those people who insist that they're living their dreams, but the problem is just that–they're their dreams. If personal goals aren't in line with your life's purpose, then you're simply wasting your time, and your life. There are millions who waste their talents on the wrong dreams. They might make mad money, but they're miserable and unfulfilled. What's the purpose in that?

Finally, there are those that don't allow their environment or current state to dictate their future. There are people that dream of moonwalking on the moon and don't let the fact that they are stationed on Earth stop them. These are the kinds of people whose motivation isn't affected by successes or failures, but by a faith that surpasses human emotions.

If you can see every detail of your vision clearly, you're not dreaming big enough. Clarity can be overrated – don't be afraid to move on a maybe. Embrace the haze and enjoy the fog. It's not always about knowing how to do it. It's about the sheer will and determination to get it done. Be more afraid of not trying than the results. It's OK to not know how it'll get done as long as you know it'll get done. If all the pieces of life's puzzles could be seen, you'd abandon your faith.

Sleep-derived dreams are similar to real life dreams in that the minute you open your eyes, is the second your dream is ruined. Dream with your eyes closed because faith requires you can't see what's in front of you, but you have to know that it's there. No need to fear the future, just look back and see how you were taken care of in the past. Today is the tomorrow you were anxious about yesterday. Don't measure Wednesday's worries with Tuesday's doubt. Relax. Most of your concerns won't matter in thirty days. Keep living. Have some faith.

Manners won't save you–your faith will.

Grace Under Fire

Grace Under Fire: Socially Awkward
Keeping Cool

No one is immune to uncomfortable or stressful scenarios. Often, what makes an experience uncomfortable is the lack of knowledge in regards to addressing it or our fear of being judged. What makes a situation stressful is your reaction to it, so in essence you create your own stress. Throw all of that crap out of the window and let's address some uncomfortable scenarios head-on. You'll never get over what you're unwilling to face.

When is it appropriate to let someone you are dating know that you are celibate?
Your celibacy deserves a round of applause. In no way should you be embarrassed by or ashamed of it.

It seems nowadays, your best bet is to tattoo *celibate* on your forehead or throw it on your online bio. Well, not quite. Your social network is public, but your sexual network doesn't have to be. Touching bodies can be a touchy subject, and if you're not the touchy feely type, then discussion of formal fornication can get awkward. I know from experience. I somehow held onto my virginity by choice throughout all of high school and some of college. That's like five decades in man-years.

You should have a defined plan for your sex life. If you don't, that's OK. I've come up with *8 Perfect Moments To Let Him Know Your Status*:

- o **Whenever you feel comfortable:** You have the right to be conservative with your sexuality. Tell him if and when you decide. You don't owe anyone an answer and your privacy must be respected. If there's no real reason he should know, then you have the right to remain silent. But anything you say or do can be used against you. Don't lead on.

o **Right away:** The "what are you looking for in a relationship" question is bound to arise. If it doesn't, then bring it up. Both of you have the opportunity to be upfront about general expectations, needs and desires. If you're not having sex, say so. If you're just looking to have fun, say so. Now, get on with the date.

o **Date three:** Right away may be too soon for some. Date one is just a pop quiz and date two is the test. By date three, you at least know you're interested in seeing this person more than twice. At that point, you can open up. Figuratively, not literally.

o **When we attempt intimacy or discuss anything intimate:** And by intimate, I mean cupping of the buttock, extended hugs accompanied with slow smiles, tongue tussling, etc. When we lead into hints about getting physical, it's an opportunity for you to speak up. This method lets us know where you stand on the subject without you having to plaster your choice on a billboard.

o **When *after-the-date* plans come up:** "So what are you about to do?" is translation for, "Can I go to your place or will you come back to mine?" That's the perfect opportunity for you to state your standards. A standard answer – "Me and my vagina are going home, alone." Smile ☺.

271

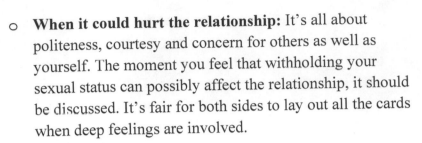

○ **When it could hurt the relationship:** It's all about politeness, courtesy and concern for others as well as yourself. The moment you feel that withholding your sexual status can possibly affect the relationship, it should be discussed. It's fair for both sides to lay out all the cards when deep feelings are involved.

○ **When discussing your faith**: If you're abstaining for religious reasons, you can casually incorporate it in the dialogue without feeling pressured. Mention it, sip your tea and move on. An appropriate way to bring up religion on a dinner date is to ask us to pray over the meal.

○ **In authentic dialogue**: As long as you're being yourself, a man will pick up on your vibe. It's when you pretend to be someone you're not that causes issues. Avoid sexual flirting or inviting a guy over after the date if you have no intimate intentions. To some, sex is as much of a deal breaker as religion. What's important to someone else should be as respected as what's important to you.

If you wait until his pants are off, you've waited too long. Communication is key. Communicate clearly and concisely. "I'm abstinent" could mean "I'm open to it, but scared," "I want to wait until marriage," "I want to do it with the right person," "I don't want kids or an STD," or "I'm just not having sex with you." Be honest. Ideally you don't want anyone surprised in the heat of the moment, so try to stay away from sexual scenarios altogether.

Ideally, you want to be with someone who wants to be with you. And wanting to be with you includes respecting you and your values. If telling him you're a virgin will scare him off, perhaps you should tell him you're a virgin. If he never calls you again, you know exactly what he wanted from you. Do not sweat it – he did you both a favor.

When is it OK to bring up the commitment conversation? Should you wait for him to bring it up?

As soon as you're done reading this! If you wait for him or for the right time, you might be waiting forever. "Someday" isn't on the calendar. Let him know your desires and intentions. He might be comfortable with things exactly the way they are. Maybe he's not ready. Or he might agree with your relationship goals and be on one accord. Be prepared for any of these reactions. Waiting for him to speak on it is a death sentence. Relationships work best when you establish boundaries upfront and communicate standards early. Speak now or hold your peace.

Should I tell a friend her/his breath is a disgrace?

Absolutely. If you have a friend who consistently has harsh breath and you don't inform that friend, you are without a doubt their enemy. A way to get the message across without coming off as rude is to simply offer gum or a mint...every time they come around. If a mint won't give the hint, pull your friend to the side and address the issue without making a scene. Get it over with and laugh about it later. A pretty smile is ruined by abusive breath. Hold your hand to your mouth and smell your own breath prior to an ill assumption that anyone else wants to.

What's the best way to answer prying questions like, "How much do you make?" or "How much did that cost you?" if you don't really want to answer the question with specifics?

As long as rude people exist, rude questions will continue to exist. Now for the easy part: What you make is no one's business but yours. A great way to respond to someone who asks you how much money you make is by simply saying, "Enough," or "I'm comfortable." This politely allows you to answer their question without a numerical value, but also let's the *Curious George* know that your salary is private. If the inquiry serves a real purpose (a friend interested in your career and curious about the salary), feel free to provide them a range. If someone asks how much something costs you, tell them you don't recall, but feel free to refer them to the store's website.

How to handle annoying co-coworkers who play their music too loudly, constantly eat foul food in the office or just talks too much.

Desperate times call for desperate measures. If someone plays music too loudly and you don't feel like dealing with that person, take it to a higher up (manager/boss) and let that person dissolve the scenario while you maintain anonymity. If you'd like to handle it yourself, offer them some headphones. If a coworker eats smelly food, bring an air freshener. If someone talks too much, don't give him or her the chance to talk to you. Make your office space as non-intrusive as possible. Stack a pile of blank papers on your desk to show you're busy. Pick up the phone every time they walk by. Do anything to symbolize busyness.

You text someone a really personal message and realized it went to the wrong person.

If they don't respond, act like it never happened and they'll likely do the same. If you do get a response, reply with a simple, "Wrong person," text. We all make mistakes, but always double check before you text. Some phones offer delayed texting that allows up to five seconds for you to cancel a message before it goes through.

Running into an ex with his new girlfriend.

Always play it casually. Don't draw unnecessary attention to the scene. Be cordial and leave it at that. No sense in making a potentially awkward situation worse. Besides, an ex is an example of what to never do again. You should be in a space where seeing them happy doesn't affect you.

Your significant other has gained a few pounds and it's turning you off. You've gently mentioned it before, but he didn't get the hint. What's the best way to have that conversation?

Don't insult or discourage him. Suggest working out together because you want to live more healthily and would like him to be there for companionship and encouragement. This approach diminishes embarrassment, finger-pointing and resentment. Teamwork makes that dream work.

You find out your friend's longtime ex is interested in you. You've always found him attractive, but didn't care to give any thought to it. What do you do?

I'll have to break this down. There are several variables to consider with a topic like dating a friend's ex. The question remains, is it ever OK to do it? Yes, it's OK. When you move out of a home, you no longer hold the key to the house. Regardless of what memories you have invested in that home, anyone, including your friend, is allowed to purchase and move in. The same holds true for relationships. Exes are fair game. Once it's been decided to move on, you are officially releasing that person out into the world. Having a sense of entitlement to an ex is like getting fired from a job and still expecting pay!

The eligibility pool of gentlemen has been dwindling, so dating a friend's ex may be closer to reality than you think. Sometimes life is simply about ration versus emotion and you can't solely live life according to feelings – you have to live life according to truth. If you've moved on, but have harbored feelings for an ex, take that up with God, not your friend interested in dating him. When you deal with the real issue of personal insecurities and truly letting go, you'll be able to see your friend with an ex, smile and move on with no further thought. If it's a recent breakup, or was a serious relationship, the wounds might take longer to heal, but the fact is they must heal. When you let go of something, someone is going to pick it up–and that someone could be a friend.

If you're the one deciding to date your friend's ex, certainly approach her about it before making the decision. If you've decided you're going to go for him, understand you're taking a risk whether she consents or not. You must determine if the risk is truly worth it. Also, try your best to ensure that the ex isn't only interested in dating you simply to spite your friend and stir up drama. If your friend asks your permission to date your ex, it's up to you to be completely honest with yourself and with her. You have no right to be upset if she asked and you said you don't care. On the contrary, if she does mind, it would be commendable of you to honor her feelings. Sacrificing your own free will for the love of another is the greatest act of love. Be willing to give up *recycled dating* when it matters. Sometimes going green isn't the healthiest option.

Interlude
Problems + Solutions

Problems: Solutions

Problem: When the handle lock on the gas pump is broken. Ugh!
Solution: Position gas cap in place of lock and you're good to go.
NOTE: Any woman accompanied by a gentleman should never
have to pump her own gas.

Problem: Running out of money at a restaurant.
Solution: This should never happen. No, really, if this does happen
to you, use your credit card, but you should always carry enough
cash to pay for two dinners. If you're alone and it happens, phone a
friend who can electronically transfer money into your account, or
even meet you at the restaurant to bail you out. Just know that you
owe that friend a favor...and the cost of the meal!

If it happens in the company of a guest and you intentionally
arrived broke, you should be ashamed of yourself. You have no
class like a student on the weekend. But like a dropout, you aren't
concerned with class. Read this book again and study the lessons
carefully. Good try. Come back soon!

If it was an honest mistake, don't be embarrassed. Ask if your
guest will graciously cover you and offer to pay that person back
upon departure.

If your date is the one who happens to give you a run for your
money...erase his number! I'm only kidding. Treat him as, or
better, than you'd want to be treated in the same scenario. A
gentlewoman should have access to an emergency fund at all
times.

Problem: Your friend's husband or significant other flirts with you.

Solution: Well, well, well. Isn't this a common occurrence? Harmless flirting is harmless. Aggressive flirting is dangerous and an obvious sign that this guy is shady and not to be trusted. It's a sensitive issue and sometimes difficult to make your friend aware of her man's transgressions. Some women are immediately defensive and might even look at you as the perpetrator. Only mention it to her if you really think it's something she needs to know. Don't cause a marriage to be ruined over something that might not be as serious as you think it is. Use discernment and stop being a hater…I'm only kidding! Friends first.

Problem: Declining an invitation to be a bridesmaid.

Solution: Weddings are expensive. Being in one is expensive as well. But you can't put a price tag on friendship. However, you can put a price tag on strangers. It's not uncommon to be invited to a bridal party of someone you just met, hardly even know or simply don't like. Etiquette has its limits. You don't have to always sacrifice yourself for the comfort of people. Here's what you do:

- Be honest. Let the bride know whatever your issue is. Speak in love and with compassion, but tell your truth…in person.
- Ask for a smaller role in the wedding. Maybe you're just not prepared for the responsibilities. Suggest being included in a smaller capacity.
- You don't have time. Weddings are important, but sometimes other priorities take precedence. You might be taking care of an ill family member or your own health could be failing. Whatever your reason, just let her know.

Oh Sit!

Oh Sit: The Power of Class

One minute they love you, the next second they curse you. It takes years to build a great reputation and seconds to crumble it. People will look forward to tearing the new you down.

Some fools can't function without chaos – if it isn't wrong, then it isn't right. And the same people who frantically cheer you on from the sidelines are the same ones anticipating your fall from grace. They feed off of controversy and gossip only as long as it doesn't involve them.

Expect to be met with resistance. You'll be a greater person after the final page is turned. Not everyone will be happy for you because they're not yet happy for themselves. Lazy men will complain about your "unrealistic" standards. Unfulfilled women will be the first to let you know that you think you're *all that*, when in reality they think you're *all that*. Some discouragement will even be courtesy of family and "friends."

You've got a lot to celebrate! But it'll be difficult to smile surrounded by glares. It's like being driven in a limo through a recession–it's considered bad taste. Not many people enjoy seeing success through a window. When others cry, they want you to cry with them. Misery doesn't do well alone. It prefers company. This idea can challenge your humility and leave you conflicted.

As a result, you'll hold back. You won't share all of your victories or speak of the details. You'll even withhold wins from your friends. Your completed checklist looks like a lot of other's to-do lists. You might begin to get uncomfortable when you begin to receive more and more attention. When you get praise, you'll pass it right back. There will be an urge to downplay everything. It'll be your way of keeping level and staying humble.

It's not wise to throw success in people's faces while society suffers. But life throws difficulty at everyone. No one is exempt. Sometimes getting through the world's challenges and coming out on top commands applause. Sometimes champagne is necessary and a pat on the back is earned, even if there's a war is going on outside. It's not selfish to be happy! Let others know when you display your joy, it's not arrogance–it's you giving glory to God. Sorry that upsets you.

Adjust to the hate. Have empathy for the envious. For they know not what they do. Some people's security is their insecurity. They don't feel good about themselves unless they feel bad about others. Scandal is in style. Gossip is therapy for the insecure.

The goal isn't for everyone to love you – the goal is for you to love everyone.

While others hurl insults, just love them. Keep on being the best version of successful you can. No one can *drive* you crazy unless you give up the *keys*. No one said this would be easy, but it'll be worth it.

When someone dies, a baby is born. There is life after death. Yell, shout and scream–celebrate in between. And when they say women are best kept quiet, ask who the hell "they" are. You always hear about "they," but never see them! Your voice is in your actions. Your words are more powerful when your deeds match them. People will *run* their mouths–but you *run* your empire. Go ahead and have a seat…on your throne.

You were once afraid of people saying, "Who does she think she is?" Now is your time to show them.

Tilt your crown!

Still a Lady

Still a Lady: Flaws and All

At the end of it all…

You'll laugh, you'll cry, you'll get mad and you'll mess up. You're still going to swear. If your hand gets jammed in a door, you're not going to yell, "Ah shucks!" just because you read this book. When you close this book, you'll forget to compliment a stranger or tell somebody, "Thank you." You're going to date a few more of the wrong people before getting it right and you just might get married…and divorced. Insecurity can still seep in. You're human. You're a gentlewoman. You're not perfect and you won't ever be. If you were flawless, people would complain about how perfect you are. Perfection won't prevent patronizing. But you're someone's perfect fit and deserve to be treated as such. A diamond uncut, unset and unclean is still a diamond.

The focus isn't always avoiding wrong. Everyone has done wrong and will continue to mess up. The focus is how to recover from that wrong and make better choices in the future. People often focus on the problem, the cause prevention – all of which are good. But they neglect the solutions and the recovery. Figure it out. After every storm, the sun has no choice but to shine. Tough times amplify awareness of God's presence – embrace them. You've got a good soul. Defend it. Cherish it. Live in such a way that if anyone should speak badly of you, no one would believe it

Reading this book and consuming its invaluable scribing is the perfect step toward beauty. You've received the information, now what are you going to do about it?

Die an old Lady with no regrets and keep on wearing your crown.

The Beginning

The Beginning: *Crown*

"There will come a time when you believe everything is finished; that will be the beginning." -Louis L'Amour

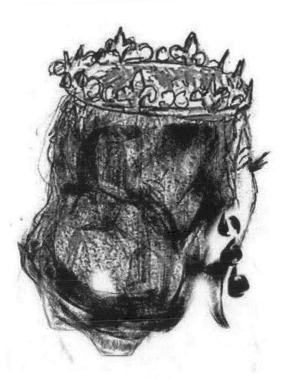

Your journey is a pleasure to watch!

Diligence is excellence over time. Excellence is easy. Doing it over time isn't. However, you never grew weary in well doing. You didn't focus on those passing you by. They grew tired. You paid no attention to those crossing the finish line. They all failed to realize there were more laps to go. You respected the process even when you had to go at it alone. This success was a sacrifice. You were

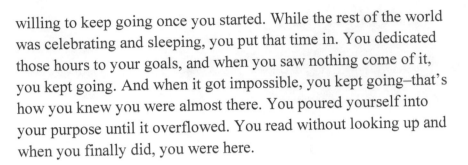

willing to keep going once you started. While the rest of the world was celebrating and sleeping, you put that time in. You dedicated those hours to your goals, and when you saw nothing come of it, you kept going. And when it got impossible, you kept going–that's how you knew you were almost there. You poured yourself into your purpose until it overflowed. You read without looking up and when you finally did, you were here.

I've been expecting you. I've anticipated your arrival. It's with great pride that I welcome you to the other side. Allow me to reintroduce you:

She is the calm amid the chaos.

Don't use this wisdom to bring forth destruction. Refrain from using this knowledge to degrade men. Instead use this book as an ally. Let it speak for you. Allow men access to it in order to gain a deeper understanding and appreciation for women as a whole. Use this as a springboard for young women entering womanhood. Use the contents of this book as a foundation for all women. This book is yours. This is your story. It starts here. It commences now. Life must begin with a woman–a gentlewoman.

The work doesn't stop once the wisdom comes. A gentlewoman makes everything around her beautiful. Teach others by loving and by just being. You don't complain about the future; you change it. This is urgent. You can. You will. You must. All that's left for you to do is close the book, slowly tilt your chin up, put on some heels and prepare for the greatest walk of your life.

One size fits all.

Straighten your crown.

Welcome to amazing.

Fin!

... Now that we've covered gentlewomen and gentlemen,
It's time to discuss us as one...together...

Acknowledgements

It is finished. This is it! God is good. Thank you, Lord. Thank you for your faithfulness and your favor. I pray this book is used for your glory. Let it reach millions. Let these words touch lives and move through communities. Let it shift culture and impact generations. Let it tremble the world. The praise is Yours. All criticism is mine. More of you, Lord…less of me. If there is anyone reading these words that might be going through something they feel they can't get through alone, show them Your glory. Bless every reader of this book. Open the floodgates of heaven and show them Your love. TO WHOM IT MAY CONCERN: It will all work out in your favor–in Jesus name, Amen.

I used to wonder why married men always thanked their wives after every accomplishment. I get it, I get it; I swear that I get it. Thank you to my very own gentlewoman for being my muse, my lover and my best friend. Painters use models to paint. Your stroke is the cure to my writer's block. When I couldn't craft up gorgeous words to say, I thought of you. You are everything beautiful. Being your husband is by far my greatest accomplishment.

To the supporters and readers, you're the reason I write. I have a shoe-on-the-other-foot style that sets out to broaden your perspective. My words are written to give voice to the silent, the silenced and the misunderstood. My goal is for each of you to be more understanding and less judgmental while reminding you of what truth is. Thank you for giving me a shot and sticking with me. I don't consider you fans–I consider you fam.

To all the other wonderful women who helped inspire "Gentlewoman," thank you. Grandma Frettie Jackson, Arlene Amaker, Gwynne Toney, Auntie Jacque, Auntie Bolaji, Auntie

Bose, Auntie Brenda, Aunt Celeste, Mrs. Gail Bereola, Nikke Bereola, Abigail Bereola, Angela Bereola, Sheri Lawson, Baby Adanya Bereola, Lisa Bush, Cousins Cassandra & Vivian Jackson, DaNeisha Goode, Adjele Frank, Therese & Georgia Onyemem, The Swann Ladies.

I didn't do this alone. Thank you grandpa Luther Jackson (*Psalms 27*), and my daddy, Rev. Olu Bereola. I'll never be too grown to refer to you as daddy! Thank you Pops a.k.a Bruce Toney. Thanks to my diligent editor Charlina Allen Pruitt and my reviewer Latoya Smith. Both lifesavers! Thank you so much to marketing genius and good friend, Justin Huff. You pushed and inspired me throughout this process. I know you don't care for credit, but you got it! Thank you CTRL Studios, Andrew Marshall, MMI Digital Photography, Lindsay Adams, Graham Knoxx, Chenoia N. Bryant, Heather Norton, Crystal Hanes, Martha Kim, Lisa Campbell, Arie Luster, Dorien Toku, Jordyn Bullock, Gebriel Gidewon, Bai Yun, Luciana Garbarni, Keely Brembry, Arian Reed, Uncle Earl Nichols, Pastor J. Alfred Smith Jr., Allen Temple Baptist Church family, Darrell Smith, Chloe Williams, Tony Gaskins Jr., Dr. Alex Ellis, Remi Bereola, Ryan Bush, Gary Banks II who promised to contact me everyday until this book was finished...he did! Thanks to Doc, Jonathan Bullock, J. Fred III, Jerrund Wilkerson II, Framp, Johnathan McGriff, Johnnie Tangle III, Tommy Fulcher, Cheapy Ivy, Matthew Heisser, Robert Douglas, Brandon Jones, Bret Sweet, Kenneth Whalum III for providing the soundtrack to write to, Malcolm Marshall, *Street Soldiers* Radio, Mark Todd, Uncle Dwight, JQ, Hunt Jack, EluJay, Nbueke & Jit Lassey, Justice Bereola and Daijon Bereola. Thank you to my amazing endorsers Hill Harper, Michelle Williams and Congresswoman Barbara Lee.

Thank you to all those who contributed portions to the book: Meagan Good, Congresswoman Barbara Lee, Dr. Jamal Bryant, Bryan-Michael Cox, Alesha Reneé, Jerri Evans, Jaye Price, Rahman Grayson, Toye Adedipe, Bobby Wagner, Dr. Idoroenyi Anaman, Everett Frampton and Leola Bell. You've changed lives! Thanks to all those who've ever supported me!

If I forgot anyone, you know I love you. I've been working on this book for three years. I'm tired and I'm getting old! Charge it to my head, not my heart or my debit card.

Any person who has ever doubted me, thank you. Anyone who has ever told me "No," I genuinely appreciate you. Anyone who said I couldn't, I did. I hope your girlfriends have this book!

"Blessed are you when people insult you, persecute you and falsely say all kinds of evil against you because of Me." –**Matthew 5:11**

ABOUT THE AUTHOR
Enitan O. Bereola, II

As an award-winning, two-time best-selling author, celebrity ghostwriter, public speaker, etiquette impresario, Beverly Hill's relationship advice columnist and Soul Train columnist, Enitan Bereola II's voice reaches generations. He's exercised his etiquette on FOX News and dished dating advice to NBC Niteside, BET and MTV. He's a regular on California's 106.1 KMEL "Street Soldiers" radio and the author was selected as one of BLACK ENTERPRISE Magazine's Young & Bold Business Leaders. Bereola's been featured on the national covers of Equanimity, American Dreaming and Shades Wedding magazine.

The Bereolaesque brand garners interests of celebrities and pop-culture alike. He's paired up with Beats By Dre's "Show Your Color" campaign to spread his gentleman message, as well as Jay-Z and Steve Stoute's Translation, LLC advertising & marketing company. Bereola produced an international soundtrack to his first book entitled, "Seat 1-A," and the short film, "This Time," starring Reagan Gomez and Terri J. Vaughn.

Bereola has been the keynote speaker at over 50 colleges and universities. He's been invited to speak at Harvard, Stanford, Tufts and other institutions. Bermuda College and Kansas State made his book a required part of their curriculum.

Mr. Bereola partnered with the Alice E. Foster Scholarship Program through the San Jose Links, Inc. who sponsors scholarships for high school graduates exiting the foster care system. He also partnered with Autism Speaks through American Dreaming Magazine who donates 100% of profits from POP displays at retailers.
Contact: info@contemporarygentlemen.com

Outro...

It's not what a man drives, but what drives a man / So if he's driven don't drive him out just because he drives a minivan / It's up to us to be men, but please hold us accountable for being gentle / If you keep making it easy, most of us will keep right on being simple / We're not blaming you, but we both play a role / If you refused to date men who didn't work out, then we'd all be swoll / If you only liked men with birthmarks, we'd all draw moles / And if you commanded honor, we'd speak love straight to your soul / Most of us get it, we understand it / But you must first command it / Not every man is gentle and respect isn't always granted / But dammit, I can't stand it when you settle like dandruff ... you overlook what weak men do and take whatever you're handed / Chivalry isn't dead unless we are...

III

Made in the USA
Lexington, KY
02 January 2014